Looking
into
the Invisible
Intuition, Clairvoyance, Dreams

Translated from the French
Original title : REGARDS SUR L'INVISIBLE

Omraam Mikhaël Aïvanhov

Looking into the Invisible

Intuition, Clairvoyance, Dreams

3ʳᵈ edition

Izvor Collection — No. 228

P R O S V E T A

Prosveta S.A. – B.P. 12 – 83601 Fréjus Cedex (France)

ISSN 0763-2738
ISBN 2-85566-469-1
first édition: ISBN 2-85566-463-2

Readers will better understand certain aspects of the lectures published in the present volume if they bear in mind that the Master Omraam Mikhaël Aïvanhov's Teaching was exclusively oral and that the editors have made every effort to respect the flavour and style of each lecture.

The Master's Teaching is more than a body of doctrines: it is an organic whole, and his way of presenting it was to approach it from countless different points of view. By repeating certain aspects in a wide variety of contexts he constantly reveals a new dimension of the Whole and, at the same time, throws new light on the individual aspects and on their vital links with each other.

TABLE OF CONTENTS

Chapter One

THE VISIBLE AND THE INVISIBLE

If it is difficult to get human beings to accept that the unseen world is a reality, it is because the organs which would enable them to perceive and comprehend that world are still not as highly developed as the sense organs of touch, sight, hearing, smell and taste which put them in touch with the physical world.

Most men and women think that the notion of another world peopled with innumerable invisible beings that are just as real and, often, a great deal more highly evolved than those they rub shoulders with every day, is too far-fetched, too ridiculous to be taken seriously. To their way of thinking, anything that cannot be perceived by men or by one of the highly sophisticated instruments used by scientists, simply does not exist. This is very faulty reasoning. Can they see the one thing that is essential to them, their own life ? Suppose you see a man's body stretched out on the ground. He is visible ; he is tangible, but he is dead ; something invisible has left him, that something that once enabled him to walk about, to love and speak and think. You can put all the food and all the treasures of the world by his side, telling him, 'There you are, my friend : all that is for you. Enjoy it !' but it will not change anything ; you will get no reaction. In the face of this, how can anyone doubt the existence of the invisible world ?

The visible world would be nothing if it were not animated and sustained by the invisible world. We must always seek the invisible behind what is visible. If the world exists for you, if you can see the earth and the sky and the sun, it is because there is an invisible principle within you that enables you to see them through the visible instruments of your eyes. If that invisible principle were not there your eyes would be no use at all, you would not see anything with them. The visible world is simply the outer wrapping of the invisible world without which we could know nothing of what exists around us.

If people categorically refuse to acknowledge the existence of the invisible world it simply proves that they have never really thought about it. Have they ever seen the thoughts and feelings that occupy them all day and all night ? Of course they haven't, and yet it never occurs to them to doubt that these thoughts and feelings are absolutely real. Does someone who is in love doubt the existence of his love ? He cannot see it, he cannot touch it, and yet he is ready to move heaven and earth because of it. And has anyone ever seen his own conscience ? When a judge declares, 'in all conscience', that the accused is guilty, he is condemning him in the name of something he has never seen and whose very existence he calls into question : is that logical ?

Actually, although they don't realize it, human beings believe only in what is invisible, intangible. The reasons for which they think, feel, love, suffer and weep are always invisible, and yet they continue to insist that they don't believe in the invisible world. What a contradiction ! Innumerable crimes are committed simply because people take everything that goes through their minds as reality. A jealous husband suspects his wife of being unfaithful to him and, without even taking the trouble to confirm his suspicions, he kills her. A man suspects a competitor of planning to ruin him ...and one more death occurs !

People never doubt the reality of what they think and feel ; for them, it is the absolute truth. When you try to explain your own point of view, they hesitate : 'I don't know, I'll have to think about that ...I must study the question', but when it is a question of what *they* think and feel there is no need to study anything ; it is obviously the only reality. In a way they are quite right : how can anyone doubt the reality of a sensation that causes them to cry out in joy or anguish ? Inner realities are the only things that are not open to doubt. In fact, inner realities are living entities, and this is why the Initiates tell us not only that an invisible, intangible world exists, but that it is the only reality. Of course, this 'invisible world' is not entirely invisible : to Initiates it is visible, substantial and tangible, and it is peopled by creatures, currents, lights, colours, forms and scents which are far more real than those of the physical plane. Initiates know and study the realities of this world.

It would be a mistake to think that emotions, feelings and thoughts, the things of the psychic, spiritual world, cannot be studied with scientific precision. Scientists who neglect this world in the belief that the instruments needed to study it do not exist are mistaken. The necessary instruments do exist ; in fact they are far more precise and accurate than those used to measure the phenomena of the physical plane. In chemistry and physics one has to allow for a possible, almost unavoidable, margin of error. You cannot measure the weight of a substance to within one electron, for instance. Whereas in the Science of the invisible world, every electron is counted, weighed and calculated : accuracy is absolute.

Yes, life can be studied. In fact, the inner spiritual life can be known with even greater accuracy than can be achieved on the physical plane, on condition, of course, that our instruments of absolute precision, our relevant spiritual organs, have been developed. As long as we have not developed these organs, we have no right to deny the reality of the invisible world. As a matter of fact, man has not developed even his physical organs to any great extent. Some animals can see, hear, smell or sense certain odours or ultrasonic waves, certain radiations of light or signs of coming storms, earthquakes or epidemics, that man is incapable of perceiving.

The only reasonable attitude for a scientist, therefore, is to say, 'The present state of our knowledge doesn't allow us to make a definitive statement about the question : it needs a great deal more study.' Instead of this, they make all kinds of official pronouncements and are responsible for misleading mankind and, sooner or later, they are going to have to pay a heavy price for this responsibility ; it has gone on record against them and Heaven is implacable towards those who lead mankind astray. All those scientists who see themselves as a universal yardstick, the sole arbiters of truth, fail to realize that, in doing so, their own limitations become an insurmountable obstacle to any further progress, not only to their progress but to that of the whole of humanity. How is it that everybody believes travellers who come back from the other side of the world and tell of the countries they have explored, the rivers that flow through them and the people who live in them, whereas they refuse to believe those who try to tell them about the spiritual regions that they have visited ? Those who explore the physical world could be lying, and yet people believe everything they say, while they systematically doubt the word of those who explore the invisible world.

All the Sacred Scriptures of all religions speak of the existence of invisible creatures whose presence has repercussions in the lives and destinies of human beings. The Christian religion puts these beings into two categories : the spirits of light and the spirits of darkness, angels and demons. Other religions have put more emphasis on the nature spirits that dwell in the four elements. Personally, I have often spoken to you about all these entities, particularly about the Angelic Hierarchies mentioned in the Cabbalah and adopted by Christianity, so I shall not enlarge on the subject today.

For my part, I believe in the invisible world ; in fact, I believe only in that. The whole of our existence is governed and permeated by the invisible world. Even our sensations of well-being and joy — as, equally, those of pain and sorrow — are linked to the presence of invisible creatures that have been attracted to us by the way we live. You will say, 'We can't see them, so they don't exist.' Just a minute : would you ask a blind man to make a judgment about something he cannot see ? If you were clairvoyant you would see them ; you would see, for instance, that, every time you experience a great joy, throngs of winged creatures come to you, laden with gifts of light and wreathing trails of scintillating colours and delicious perfumes as they sing and dance around you. Similarly, if you were clairvoyant, you would see the horrid twisted features of the entities that delight in pulling your hair, pricking and clawing at you, when you are anxious or in distress. Esoteric tradition tells us that these are the undesirable entities that prowl round human beings looking for one that offers them the chance of some sport. And when they find one, they say, 'Aha, here's a fellow who looks promising. Let's go and torment him ; it will be fun to see him crying and wringing his hands !' Yes, this is what is happening when you are unhappy and feeling tormented.

Of course, the intellectual and medical bigwigs of the 20th century could not possibly admit that human beings are visited by benevolent or malevolent entities who come to help and console them or, on the contrary, to torment and destroy them. They think that when the functions of the human psyche are disturbed or, on the contrary, when they are enhanced, it is due to the presence of certain chemical elements. That is true, but where do these chemical elements come from ? They are simply a materialization of the benevolent or malevolent spirits that people attract to themselves. If, through their faults and failings, human beings open their doors to the spirits of darkness, these spirits will enter and play havoc with them. Psychologists and psychoanalysts have all sorts of names for the resulting disorders, but the truth is that they all have one and the same cause : the undesirable entities that have been attracted by our imperfect way of life.

These facts are fully explained in all the Sacred Scriptures of the world, and clairvoyants have seen them for themselves, but as long as men fail to develop the spiritual faculties that would permit them to become familiar with the invisible world, and as long as they go on doubting the truths taught by Initiatic Science, they will go on forming philosophies based exclusively on the testimony of their five senses and, inevitably, the conclusions they draw from these philosophies will be false.

The question of the existence of undesirable entities may seem a little clearer to you if you think about the microscopic organisms that continually threaten and kill human beings. How long is it since a biologist first found a microbe, virus, bacillus or bacterium under his microscope ? Hardly more than a century ! Before this, human diseases were attributed to the most improbable causes. At least, today, we know that illnesses are caused by these tiny living organisms, even though we may not know everything about them : the consequences of their presence — illness and death — is only too obvious. The pattern of events on the physical plane is the same as those on the astral and mental planes and here, too, the results are obvious : anxiety, mental torment, obsessions and madness. The only thing is that there are no microscopes sufficiently sophisticated to detect the virus of the astral and mental planes.

In what concerns the psychic and spiritual realms, human beings are still living in the era before Pasteur, when people refused to take any precautions against microbes that they could not see. They cannot see these undesirables — the microbes of the psychic plane — so they take no precautions against them. Perhaps, one day soon, a new Pasteur will come, with new instruments that will enable us to see the astral entities that ravage imprudent human beings. In the meantime, you would do better to admit that they exist and, above all, take measures to defend yourselves against them by leading reasonable, sensible lives.

Certain clairvoyant cabbalists have seen these undesirable entities ; they have even named them, choosing names that express exactly the characteristics of the spirits to which they are attributed by taking into account the numerical value of each letter. Although I know the names of these spirits,

I don't want to reveal them to you because I don't want you to have any point of contact with them. One needs to be extremely strong, to have a very strong aura and to know how to work with colours and light, before one can study these entities without danger. In any case, whether you believe this or not, if you are not extremely vigilant, you will be unable to prevent undesirable entities from harassing you. Why do you suppose that Jesus said, 'Watch and pray', and 'Be sober, be vigilant ; because your adversary the devil walks about like a roaring lion, seeking whom he may devour' ? Could Jesus have been saying something meaningless ? And if human beings are so well informed about the reality of everything, why are they constantly subject to trouble and distress ? The only solution is to turn back to the wisdom that has been so neglected and despised and begin, at long last, to transform your lives.

Space is filled with billions of malicious entities which have sworn to destroy mankind. To be sure, it is also filled with billions of luminous entities that are there to help and protect you, but their help and protection will never be wholly effective if you yourselves make no effort to follow the right path. Nor can a Master do anything to protect you if you persist in living unreasonably. A Master will instruct and enlighten you ; he will even try to influence you by means of his own thoughts and feelings, but if you demolish all his good work and open your doors to the entities of darkness by your own recklessness and superficiality, your own lack of goodwill, what can he do about it ?

Someone who wishes to make serious progress on the path of evolution, therefore, must begin by cultivating his sensitivity towards the invisible world. But that is no more than a preliminary condition. It is not enough to acknowledge that space and our own beings are inhabited by invisible entities and currents, we also have to exert ourselves and collaborate with them in some constructive work. Ah, yes ; the idea is new to you, isn't it ? You are accustomed to keeping things tidy on the physical plane, in your home, at work and even in your own appearance, and this is all to the good. But inwardly, in your thoughts and feelings, everything is topsy-turvy because you don't believe that your thoughts and feelings belong to a world that really exists and in which you must also work at keeping things tidy, harmonious and beautiful.

People are willing to go to almost any lengths for what is visible and, in the meantime, the invisible is forgotten and neglected. From now on, your attitude must change : the invisible world is a reality, a reality even more important than the visible world, and this means that it must be your first priority.

Once you concentrate on this inner work you will begin to feel that all the pure, luminous moments you experience bring you into contact with an infinity of other currents, other beings. When you limit your attention to the visible, material world, you limit and impoverish yourself ; you yourself become more material. Whereas, when you work with the limitless wealth and immensity of the invisible world, you forge a link between yourself and all those creative forces, all those luminous entities at work amongst the stars and constellations, all those countless worlds of the universe ; you begin to taste divine life.

Chapter Two

THE LIMITED VISION OF THE INTELLECT
THE INFINITE VISION OF INTUITION

I

Human beings reject every state of mind likely to bring them closer to the divine world, thinking that they are all abnormal or dangerous. The only thing they have any faith in is the intellect ; with the intellect, at least, you know where you are ; you can keep your wits about you.

When a teacher explains things to you in class, he uses charts and diagrams to enable you to follow his explanations step by step without losing your way. But however many charts and diagrams he uses, and however clear and logical his explanations and arguments may be, they will not prevent him from losing his head when he is out of the classroom. Although intellectuals exercise great prudence, discipline and objectivity in their professional work, they consider it normal to be entirely subjective in their everyday lives, and willingly abandon themselves to the disorder and turmoil of their passions. But it is precisely in these circumstances that they would do better to distrust their impulses and make better use of their intellect. Unfortunately, they keep all their distrust for heavenly, divinely harmonious sensations which create no turmoil and inject no harmful elements into their inner being. What a strange mentality !

If you look at the statistics, you will see that it is amongst intellectuals that the majority of cases of psychological and mental illness are to be found. The intellect is incapable of protecting man from psychological problems ; rather the opposite, in fact. Life does not consist exclusively in making observations, measuring and calculating ; human beings are not machines. We have to face up to the shocks and difficulties of existence ; we have to avoid being dragged under and destroyed by our passions ; we have to discover the underlying reality of things, and the intellect cannot cope with all this.

Of course, many of those who fancy themselves as spiritualists[1] or mystics are simply bizarre, fanatical or mentally unbalanced, and intellectuals have drawn their own conclusions from this and apply them to all spiritualists and mystics. But that is dishonest. True mystics are perfectly sensible

1 The word 'spiritualist', in the language of Omraam Mikhaël Aïvanhov, simply means one who looks at things from a spiritual point of view, whose philosophy of life is based on belief in a spiritual reality.

people : the way they behave, their thoughts, words and gestures, the way they look at one ...everything about them is composed and harmonious. Why should anyone imagine that the world of the spirit drives people out of their minds, that it is the divine world that deludes them into thinking that they can see and talk to God, face to face, or that they are Christ, the Virgin Mary or Joan of Arc ? Rather than run the risk of being caught up in such hare-brained notions themselves, many people have ended as dried-up intellectuals. But, of course, if someone embarks on the spiritual life without a guide or instructions of any kind, he can easily go out of his mind. The fact that this has often happened makes it easy to see why some people are distrustful of mysticism. The only trouble is, though, that to give absolute priority to the intellect is not the solution either.

The development of man's intellectual faculties came considerably later than those of the heart and of feeling and, by enabling him to observe, reason and understand, they give him immense possibilities for work and self-development. It would be true, in a way, to say that the intellect is related to the eyes : to see things is to begin to understand them. In fact, don't we often say, 'I see', meaning, 'I understand' ? Nature has worked for millions of years to develop the intellect, but she does not intend it to have the last word : she has plans for the development of other, far superior, faculties in man. The intellect is limited : it bases its judgments and the conclusions it draws on external appearances and on a partial view of reality.

This means that the intellect is not capable of synthesis, nor is it capable of knowing things from within and, for these reasons, it does not allow man to judge people and situations unerringly. This lack is the source of innumerable mistakes and misunderstandings. Obviously, it is possible for the intellect to accumulate a tremendous number of elements and use them to arrive at an overall view of the whole, but how long would that take ? And, even then, there would always be some subtle, intangible elements that it could never grasp. When you first meet someone, for instance, you cannot immediately know all his strengths and weaknesses or virtues ; it takes a long time before you can know all about him. The only way to know someone at once and in his totality is by intuition, for intuition is a manifestation of the spirit. Intuition does not need different elements in order to form a judgment ; it goes straight to the heart of people and things and knows them instantly and unerringly. Nothing is hidden to the eyes of intuition ; intuition alone can know the whole of reality.

If Cosmic Intelligence has endowed human beings with an intellect, it was, obviously, with the intention that they should use it. Unfortunately, they do so in such a way as to deprive themselves of other, subtler ways of exploring and gaining knowledge. They are incapable, for instance, of using their psychic faculties in order to see into the anatomy and physiology of the human body ; this is why they are obliged to dissect it. You will ask, 'What do you mean ? Is it possible to study the anatomy and physiology of an animal or a human being without cutting them open ?' Certainly, it is. Aren't there already all kinds of sophisticated instruments that enable us to see inside a human body ? And, as I have already told you so many times, all the instruments that man builds on the physical plane correspond to psychic and spiritual instruments that he already possesses within himself ; if he is obliged to build them outwardly, it is because he has not yet discovered their existence or learned to use them inwardly. I hope this is clear to you now. It is because scientists have never developed the ability to investigate matter by means of their intuitive faculties that they are obliged to tear it apart. They are like children who destroy their toys because they want to see what makes them tick. In spite of the immense pride science takes in its discoveries, it still has the mentality of a child.

Human beings are greatly handicapped by being limited to the use of the five senses and their principal representative, the intellect. When they want to explore the universe, the sun, the planets or the

centre of the earth and the depths of the ocean, they
are obliged to build all kinds of machines and, until
such time as these machines are perfect, a great
many things will remain unknown to them. And,
even if they did succeed in perfecting their machines,
the fact that it would take far longer than the normal span of a human life to reach the outer limits
of space means that they are up against yet another
limitation. By making use of the senses of the
spiritual world, on the other hand, human beings
have the power to reach any point in space and to
know everything.

Man must become more and more conscious,
therefore, that he has instruments at his disposal
that are far superior to the intellect. He must learn,
in future, to rely a little less on the intellect, to look
on it simply as an instrument for the study and ex-
ploration of matter. For, even in the simple things
of everyday life, the intellect is incapable of guiding
us : it will always lead us into error, not only because
its view of reality is incomplete but, above all,
because hidden motives of egotism and self-interest
underlie everything it does and, in the long run, this
inevitably causes problems. The intellect has no
capacity for generosity, selflessness or renunciation ;
that is not what it was designed for ; its only skill
lies in turning things to its own advantage. If, at
any time, it allows itself to be lured into making
a sacrifice or a gesture of generosity, the very next

day it regrets having been so stupid as to listen to the advice of the heart or soul.

As to the possibility of brotherhood being established amongst all men, of the world becoming one immense family, of making it possible, one day, for all mankind to live happily ...such questions are beyond its powers of conception and realization. It cannot rise high enough to discover the true means, the true remedies or solutions. Whatever solutions the intellect imagines or proposes are based on its partial and egocentric vision of reality ; this is why they are always inadequate, why they inevitably lead to misunderstandings, why nothing is ever settled and new problems keep arising. The intellect can never be a perfect instrument because it operates in the foggy, murky realms of ordinary thoughts and feelings. A clear vision of things has not been given to it, and if we rely on it too exclusively and never look any higher for the other instruments and faculties that God has given us, we shall never find the best solutions.

The time has come for you to cease being dazzled by the exploits of the intellect, to acknowledge the existence of your spiritual bodies, to study their different possibilities and work to develop your intuition. For intuition is that higher form of intelligence that belongs to the Causal plane and which, instead of being motivated by egocentric considerations, pursues a purely heliocentric, theocentric goal. In this way, instead of looking for personal advantage in everything you undertake, you will begin to put yourself in the service of God. Not that God needs anything from us : He is so immensely rich and mighty that He does not need us to work for Him. It is for our own sakes that we are asked to work for God, because that is how we learn to change our point of view and the orientation of our lives ; it is we who benefit from our work, we who begin to see improvements in ourselves. When all our energies converge on a focal point other than ourselves, all our inner processes, functions and vibrations change and, instead of being perpetually dull and drab, we become luminous and radiant.

Obviously, as I have already said, there is no question of suppressing the activity of the intellect. It is precisely because God wants man to develop all the possibilities of his brain to the fullest extent that He has sent him to earth to explore matter at first hand. But, in the course of this involution, the five senses have taken on such importance that men have lost all notion of the divine world ; they no longer have any communication with luminous entities, they never think of them any more, they can no longer even sense their presence. In spite of that, this descent into matter will always be an extraordinary acquisition for mankind. God's purpose is to bring human beings to a state of perfection in this way, by letting them experience this passage through matter, through the abyss, and by bringing them back, through disease and death, to life and resurrection, to light and absolute freedom, to the knowledge of their Creator. This ascending movement has already begun, the Heavenly currents are gradually gaining strength and greater numbers of luminous souls are coming to incarnate in the world. Before very long, we shall begin to see philosophers, artists and scientists who speak a new language, create new works of art, proclaim new values and bring with them a new vision of the world ; a new culture will spring up in every part of the world, a culture which will establish the Kingdom of God and His Righteousness. But, before they can bring this about, men must learn to work with the highly sophisticated instruments they possess, the organs of their Causal, Buddhic and Atmic bodies. In other words, they must learn to work with the spirit, for only the spirit can contemplate and comprehend the realities of the divine world.

Most people would admit the existence of a mental faculty beyond the level of reflection or reasoning : the faculty of intuition. But what exactly that

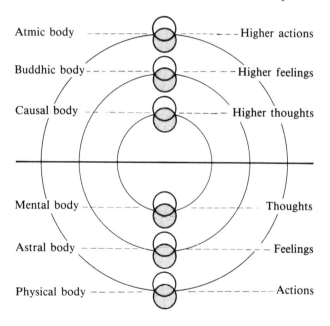

Figure 1 The six bodies of man

faculty is and how it functions is far from clear to them. In order to understand the nature of intuition, we have to refer to the diagram used by Hindus to describe the different bodies of man.

In the Hindu scheme of things, man's physical body is inhabited and animated by several subtle bodies. The subtle bodies are the astral body, seat of our feelings and emotions ; the mental body, seat of concrete ideas, that is to say, ideas that relate to matter ; the Causal or Higher Mental body which allows man access to the comprehension of sublime truths, to the mysteries of the universe ; the Buddhic body which, like the astral body, is the seat of emotions and feelings, but of a higher, divine order : universal love, self-abnegation and sacrifice. Finally, there is the Atmic body, seat of that immortal spark which is the omnipotence of God.

The first three bodies — physical, astral and mental — are fairly equally developed in all human beings, but the stage of development reached by the three higher bodies varies enormously from one individual to another. Only a certain number of philosophers and spiritualists succeed in rising to the level of the Higher Mental body and begin to live in the sublime realm of light. The brains of these few achieve such a fine degree of perfection that new centres awake into activity within their being and enable them to grasp the reality at the core of things. This is the world of intuition. Intuition is a vision, an instantaneous reception, an immediate and total grasp of the real, veritable world which lies beyond the mental plane, for, even on the mental plane, error and illusion are still possible.

The only way you can reach this world of intuition is by practices of the highest spirituality. First of all you must have a high ideal ; secondly, and this is most important, you must have a Master to give you the guidance you need in order to follow this difficult path. Finally, you must be strong willed and determined to practise tirelessly until you are sufficiently developed to perceive and grasp the realities of the sublime regions.

Intuition is a form of intelligence very different from ordinary intelligence. Of course, those who work hard with the intellect achieve a certain understanding of things but they barely graze the surface of this world of intuition in which knowledge is instantaneous and total ; it takes them years and years of research, reflection and calculations to make their discoveries. Those who have chosen the way of the spirit, on the other hand, can tune in directly to these sublime regions, on condition, of course, that they stop living in a turmoil of emotions and passions that prevents them from seeing things clearly, and introduce order into every part of their being. Only in this state of peace and harmony can man attain the realm of intuition and, when he achieves this, he is like the still surface of a crystal-clear lake in which the heavens are reflected.

You will ask, 'But what use is the intellect, then ?' The intellect is extremely useful for it takes you a good part of the way. The only thing is that, once it reaches a certain point, it cannot take you any further. It says, 'We've come to a region in which I can be of no more use to you : I can't go any further. I've brought you this far ; now you need other forces, other faculties and other entities to take you by the hand and show you the way.' Isn't this exactly what happens on earth ? You begin by driving to the station in a car ; next, you board a train. When the train has taken you as far as it goes, you continue your journey by boat. After a certain number of hours or days, you have to leave the boat too, but a plane is waiting for you and, in no time at all, you are able to continue your journey by air. The analogy is easy to understand : the intellect will take you only so far on your inner journey ; it cannot take you all the way.

The intellect is an extraordinarily useful tool when it comes to preparing conditions, clearing the way, getting everything ready and in place while waiting for intuition to manifest itself. It helps you to watch and control what goes on in your head and your heart, to eliminate thoughts and feelings that are negative while nurturing and amplifying those that are constructive and beneficial. Once you have succeeded, in this way, in filling your being with peace and purity — the indispensable conditions for making contact with Heaven — other currents will come and carry you to the divine realms of infinite light and absolute knowledge and, instantaneously, you will be given revelations. For this is what intuition is : a spark, a flash of light, an inner knowledge that suddenly imposes itself, without your knowing how or where it came from. All you know is that you have an absolute certainty about something. The truths, the knowledge, received through intuition are complete and infallible.

Intuition, therefore, is superior to the intellect in the same way as the speed and infallible accuracy of a computer are superior to the speed and accuracy of the brain. To be sure, the human brain is superior to a computer : it is the brain that builds the computer, feeds data into it, switches it on and gives it commands to execute. The response of the machine will always depend on the capacity of the human intelligence that supplies the data and, as that human intelligence is necessarily limited, the response will also be limited. But when you want a rapid answer about a very complex calculation or operation, a computer will give it to you in only a few seconds, whereas a human brain would take several hours or even days to reach the same result.

I have used this example of a computer simply to illustrate the fact that intuition, too, can give you answers instantaneously, without your knowing why or how the Heavenly entities that answered you were willing to do so, or what means they used. It is as though another being dwelt within you, a being who is capable of seeing the total reality of things and of communicating what it sees to you, taking into account not only the physical elements but also all those invisible, subtle elements that are beyond human understanding. Intuition, therefore, is a revelation of a higher order, beyond the reach of the intellect, and man can rise to that region only through meditation, persistent work and prayer. When you succeed in introducing peace and order into your being, the whole of Heaven will be reflected from the transparent surface of your consciousness.

The instruction that human beings are given in schools encourages them to rely far more on the intellect than on intuition. That is all well and good, but the problem is that it would take the intellect thousands of years to see and touch and comprehend the reality of the divine world or the existence of invisible entities. Intuitive minds, on the other hand, those who work with the methods of the Initiates, have no need to reflect and grope their way for centuries in order to perceive, to feel and touch reality.

It is good to have some practical contact with the world of intuition in your everyday life. This is why, when you have a serious problem to solve, try to find a quiet place in which you can concentrate. Rise, mentally, as high as you can and, when you sense that you have reached a higher plane, ask the question that is troubling you, then wait, in peace, for the answer ; there will always be an answer. The clarity of the answer you receive will depend on your level of development and on the work you have done. It may be no more than a vague sensation that is difficult to interpret, but even that will be an indication. If it is not clear, don't give up, try to make contact with the world of light and ask your question again : you will soon receive an inner light, a feeling of certainty that will tell you, without a doubt, exactly what you must do. The more highly developed a person is, the clearer and more detailed the response he receives.

Some people have the gift of clairvoyance, they see forms, colours and entities, but clairvoyance is not the highest level of investigation. The highest level is to perceive and understand things intuitively, without seeing forms or colours or anything else. Intuitive knowledge is an immediate and absolute certitude. A great many people who see forms and colours are unable to interpret them correctly, so what good does it do them to be clairvoyant ? Intuition, on the other hand, is a blending of intelligence and sensitivity, and the knowledge it gives is full and complete ; it is in this sense that intuition is superior to clairvoyance, for clairvoyance is simply the ability to see the objective aspect of the astral and mental planes. When you are clairvoyant, you see things that can either terrify you or fill you with wonder, your feelings are moved, but you receive neither knowledge nor understanding.

A true spiritualist is not interested in what he sees on the astral plane ; that is not the goal of his work, he goes beyond that level to find answers on a higher plane. Once he has received an answer through intuition, he may return to the regions of clairvoyance and clairaudience, but he must begin by aiming for the higher goal, otherwise the visions and images floating on the lower planes will prevent him from going higher ; they will cling to him and hold him down for, in these regions, everything is confused and mixed up. The images encountered here are so terrible that one cannot pursue one's ascent in peace, one is forced to mark time on this level and, in this way, one can even compromise one's evolution. This is why, as long as you do not have the power to defend yourself against these dangers, you would do better to pass through these regions with your eyes closed and begin by working to develop your intuition.

There are many different methods that you can use to develop your intuition : exercises of concentration, visualization and contemplation can all help. You can also concentrate on your higher Self and imagine that it tells you about all that it sees and knows. But, I repeat, the most effective and least dangerous method is to work at becoming pure and totally disinterested and never to be prejudiced or act out of self-interest ; only in these conditions can the obstacles to clear vision melt and fade away, only in this way will you ever come to know the reality of people and things.

Chapter Three

THE ENTRANCE TO THE INVISIBLE WORLD : FROM YESOD TO TIPHARETH

I

There are various avenues to choose from in order to enter the invisible world, and meditation and prayer are amongst the most accessible. But meditation requires preparation. If someone who has never acquired any inner discipline tries to meditate, he will begin by wandering about in the lower regions of the astral plane and stirring up these murky layers and the entities which inhabit them and which are often hostile to human beings. In this way he may become a prey to strange visions that have nothing to do with the subject of his meditation.

Before trying to meditate one must begin by putting one's psychic life in order, otherwise, even such a useful, salutary exercise as this can be dangerous, and people who have mediumistic capacities are particularly vulnerable in this respect. One must never embark on the path of spirituality

without taking some preliminary precautions. A
spiritualist has to pacify, domesticate and orientate
all his inner tendencies ; he must have only one goal,
that of reaching perfection, of obtaining wisdom
and purity, of attaining to truth. This lofty goal acts
as a kind of tuning fork : when all the particles of
his being vibrate in unison with it they will be in
harmony and his experiences in the invisible world
will be truly beneficial. In any other conditions
spirituality becomes a risky venture. You must not
imagine that any Tom, Dick or Harry can wander
in and out of the invisible world at will : it is the
home of innumerable creatures who resent intruders. It is as though you were to wander off into
a jungle : you would be in danger from any number
of man-eating beasts or poisonous snakes and
insects that live there, and, if you didn't know how
to defend yourself, you would be at their mercy.

You will say, 'But how is that possible ? Surely, if I really want to make contact with Heaven,
every experience should be beneficial ?' I'm afraid
that that is not so ; those who try to penetrate the
divine world without any previous preparation are
running a serious risk : the entities of light will not
tolerate intruders who try to enter their world,
bringing with them all the filth and stench of earth ;
they repulse them and declare war on them. No one
can do violence to the spiritual world. If you want
to approach the Heavenly entities, you must prepare

yourself by adopting an attitude of sacred respect. If you ask the sublime entities to allow you to enter their regions in order to admire their purity and to glorify the Lord, then, to be sure, you will win their friendship ; they will no longer repulse or combat you.

Unfortunately, human beings are taught no respect ; on the contrary, they are taught to be rude and violent with other people — apparently this is the best way to get along in life — and their attitude is the same towards the spirits of light. Far from recognizing that it would be so much better to win their friendship and trust by an attitude of humility and respect and by practising the virtues, they try to impose themselves at all costs. They present themselves just as they are, in the belief that Heaven is bound to accept them. But that is not what happens ; Heaven turns them away and refuses to let them in, and when you are turned away from the realm of the spirits of light, it is time to be very much on your guard, for you fall immediately into the regions of the spirits of darkness, where you will be warmly welcomed as a juicy morsel for them to feast upon.

The study of the Sephirotic Tree, which represents both the different regions of the universe and the different psychic regions in man, will help you to understand the route man must follow in order to have access to the invisible world. The first

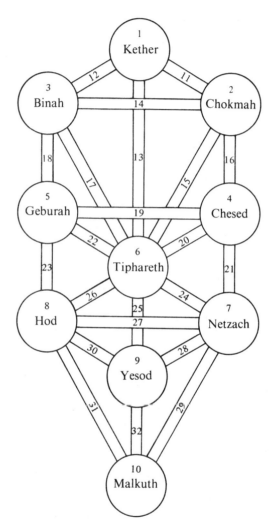

Figure 2 The Sephirotic Tree

Sephirah, counting from the bottom, is Malkuth, and Malkuth represents the physical plane, the earth. Above Malkuth is Yesod, the region of the moon, and beyond Yesod is Tiphareth, the region of the sun. When we leave Malkuth, we leave the physical plane and enter the psychic plane, Yesod. Yesod is the beginning of the psychic life and, in this sense, it represents a step up in relation to Malkuth, the physical plane. But the psychic life begins in regions of mist and of vague, indistinct forms : these are the lower regions of Yesod which have not yet been touched by the light of Tiphareth, the Sun, reason, the spirit.

The region of Yesod is far subtler than Malkuth, but the lower part, closest to Malkuth, is still too humid and misty and too full of dust ; this is the region of illusions and aberrations. It is important, therefore, to pass through this region rapidly and go beyond it to discover the world of light, Tiphareth, the region of the sun, for only in this higher region does true spiritual work begin. A great many so-called spiritualists, clairvoyants or mystics, have spent long years floundering in the lower reaches of Yesod, simply because they lacked the knowledge that would have enabled them to keep moving on until they found the light ; this is why so many of them have come to a bad end.

All those who have attempted to venture into the spiritual world without proper preparation have come face to face with that terrifying being which Initiatic Science calls the Guardian of the Threshold. In point of fact, this terrible being is in themselves : it is formed by the accumulation of all their lower tendencies, their lust, sensuality, aggressiveness, etc., and it stands in their way and forbids them to enter the higher regions until they have earned the right to do so.

In his novel, *Zanoni*, Bulwer Lytton tells of the trials of a disciple, Glyndon, who, being too impatient to wait until he was properly prepared before trying to gain access to the mysteries, disobeys his Master, Mejnour, and inhales the elixir that was supposed to give him omniscience and immortality. After a few seconds of ecstasy, he sees this hideous apparition, the Guardian of the Threshold, and falls to the ground in a swoon. Subsequently he abandons all his work as a disciple and wanders wretchedly over the face of the earth, pursued, for years, by that horrible vision until, at last, Zanoni delivers him from his torment.

One day, each one of you is going to have to meet and face up to the Guardian of the Threshold ; he is there, in the ninth Sephirah, Yesod, ready to show his terrifying face to the presumptuous disciple who dares to venture into the spiritual regions without having worked sufficiently to cultivate purity, self-mastery and courage. Only he who is armed with knowledge and who has succeeded in overcoming all his lower instincts can vanquish the Guardian of the Threshold. Then, one glance is enough : 'Go !', and the creature disappears, leaving the way open.

II

By day, when the sun is shining, we can see the objects around us and get a fairly accurate idea of their shape, colour and size and their distance from us, etc. The sun reigns over all that is clear and transparent, and from its light comes a knowledge of things as they are.

By night, on the contrary, even if the moon is shining, objects are immersed in a kind of twilight and seem to be other than what they are : something ugly may seem beautiful, whereas something beautiful may appear to be ugly and distorted. In this hazy, indistinct atmosphere it is not possible to have a clear vision of reality. Such an atmosphere affords ample scope, on the other hand, for the imagination, and imagination is also a form of vision, a form of vision that belongs to a level beyond the physical plane.

The sun, therefore, is the realm of clear knowledge and reason, and the moon is the realm of the imagination and of mediumship. In point of fact, the moon has many different aspects, but to make things simpler we only need to speak about two of them : a misty, twilight region of illusions, strange fancies, aberrations and insanity, and a region of clarity, the region of poetic imagination and true inspiration. Many artists are content with the twilight regions of the moon ; they take pride in conveying an element of unreality through their creations, something dream-like, strange and fantastic. But this hazy, indistinct universe in which they seek refuge is very dangerous and many of them go out of their minds, commit suicide or end their days as alcoholics.

To the extent to which artists live and work on the astral plane, which is higher than the physical plane, they are seers, and this is a sign of progress. But it only constitutes true progress for someone who is not content to stagnate on the lower levels ; the lower astral plane should be no more than a passageway, an avenue of approach to the higher level that is open to the influence of the sun. Unfortunately, many artists are incapable of going on to that higher level — or, at any rate, they make no effort to do so. In spite of the fact that their books, paintings and music are the expression of the lower astral plane, the dark face of the moon, they firmly believe that they are contributing something very precious to mankind, whereas it is just the opposite : their influence is extremely detrimental to mankind because they are not truly enlightened. They have considerable gifts and talents, to be sure, but they do not possess the solar elements which, alone, are capable of leading human beings to the regions of certainty, peace and light.

Of course, in one way, we can never escape from the lower regions of the astral plane because they exist within us. They are outside, but, also, inside us. Night and day exist ; the sun and the moon exist. We can't just get rid of the night or of the moon, but it is better not to expose ourselves to their influence more than need be. We have to study the moon, but we should be very wary of what it represents on the inner level in the way of philosophy or of a conception and perception of things.

So, try not to be attached to art forms which tie you to a twilight world, for not only will they not help you to see things clearly or to advance in any way, but they will prevent you from evolving. Obviously, no one can deny that the astral world is full of enchantments, but those who linger there never get any further, their evolution is arrested. This is the symbolic meaning of the passage in the *Odysseus* in which Homer describes how Ulysses stopped up his sailors' ears with wax so that they would not be seduced by the sweet voices of the

Sirens as they sailed past their island, for these creatures were known to lure sailors to their shores in order to devour them. Sirens are just one of the many symbols for the entities of the astral plane — and a great many artists have fallen prey to them !

Like Ulysses, a genuine instructor who knows the reality of things, tries to alert his disciples to the snares of the astral plane and lead them beyond it, to greater heights, where they may discover the only realities worth discovering : the splendours of the divine world, Tiphareth, the region of the sun, where everything is transparent and luminous.

Chapter Four

CLAIRVOYANCE :
ACTIVITY AND RECEPTIVITY

More and more people, nowadays, are interested in such things as mediumship, clairvoyance and telepathy, and would like to develop these faculties in themselves, thinking that it would be a great advantage to be able to know and delve into the unknown. It is true : it can be very advantageous, but it is also very dangerous. Why dangerous ? Because, in order to be clairvoyant, in order to be a medium, one is obliged to maintain an extremely passive, receptive attitude. It is because they have this attitude of passivity that clairvoyants can be messengers of the invisible. But when one is too receptive, one is like a sponge ; one absorbs everything, the good with the bad ; this is where the danger lies.

The invisible world is not empty and it is dangerous to venture into it without preparation, for not all the entities that inhabit it are luminous, some of them are malicious and hostile to human beings, and they are more than ready to lead them into error or persecute them. The invisible world also contains many monstrous creatures created by the thoughts and feelings of criminals and black magicians, and these creatures are always ready to sneak in to a human being whenever they find an open door, that is to say, whenever they find someone too weak or too ignorant to defend himself. Psychiatric hospitals are full of people whose eagerness to make contact with the invisible world through their gifts of clairvoyance and mediumship led to their being invaded by these creatures of darkness.

Mediumistic faculties belong to the feminine principle ; this is why those who possess them should take care to develop their masculine qualities as well, so as to be able to defend themselves. The history of Antiquity is full of tales of prophetesses and female seers and soothsayers, and their role was considerable. But these seers were always under the protection of high priests or Initiates, for an Initiate is someone who has developed, first and foremost, the masculine qualities of will and mastery. A true Initiate is a magus rather than a clairvoyant ; he is concerned with acting on other beings, on the elements and the forces of nature. He may have gifts of receptivity, but, more importantly, he has powers of action ; this is why he is less vulnerable than a clairvoyant. Being active and dynamic, he projects forces capable of counteracting any dangers that may threaten him. Perfection, of course, lies in developing both aspects to the full : to be both passive and emissive.

Each of us can only attract to himself the currents and entities that have an affinity with his own inner state. This is a law : man can relate only to that which corresponds to his vibrations, to his aura ; if he is not pure, luminous and strong, therefore, he will have to suffer the impact of all that is negative, unhealthy and violent in his psychic environment. People such as mediums, who are receptive and passive, are particularly vulnerable in this respect ; this is why I advise you, if you have mediumistic tendencies, not to give them a free rein until you have worked to achieve a degree of purity and inner elevation sufficient to enable you to withstand attack by the forces of darkness. Begin by making the effort to rise to a higher plane, to create a bond with light and to project that light round about you : once you sense that you are capable of doing this, and not before, you can let yourself go and become receptive, because, then, you will be protected by the work you have done to prepare yourself and by all that light that radiates from you and repulses undesirable entities.

People who are very sensitive are also, very often, extremely vulnerable, because they have not learned how to develop their spiritual defences at the same time as their sensitivity : they are incapable of doing battle ; they don't know how to go about it. A great many people believe that all they have to do in order to be visited by God is to abandon themselves to some vague mystical impulse. Not at all : if you are content to be passive there is no guarantee that it will be God who visits you ; you are more likely to be visited by some devils who have been wandering about, looking for a home, and who are only too delighted to find such a spineless, apathetic creature without defences in which to lodge.

Whatever you want to do in life you have to begin by seeing that conditions are right. If you want to pour some liquid into a container, you make sure, first of all, that it is not dirty : if it is, you wash it. And if you, yourself, are a dirty container, do you imagine that Heaven is going to pour blessings into you ? Do you imagine that the Holy Spirit would be willing to take up His abode in a swamp ? The only beings to enter you will be entities of impurity and darkness because it is they that are attracted by the food you have to offer : your uncontrolled passions and instincts. To be sure, the Holy Spirit may come to you, one day, but only when you have worked sufficiently to prepare a tabernacle fit to receive Him.

We know only too well the terrible disorders that afflict those who thought that they could receive the

Holy Spirit without preparing themselves properly. They think that they are visited by the Holy Spirit when they roll on the ground in a fit, gesticulating wildly and uttering inarticulate cries (which, they say, is 'speaking in tongues'). What a conception they must have of the Holy Spirit ! Their Holy Spirit is not even a good pedagogue since he speaks a language that no one else can understand. He may be a great polyglot but he's no pedagogue, for a pedagogue seeks, above all else, to make himself understood. How can anyone possibly imagine that the Holy Spirit, this Cosmic Principle of all wisdom and power, would choose to manifest Himself in this grotesque way, by throwing people to the ground in order to speak through them ? When you have something to say to a friend, or to your husband or wife, do you roll about on the ground shrieking, in the hope of convincing them ? You don't ? Then your inspiration is more reliable than that of all those people who claim to be visited by the Holy Spirit.

If you really want to communicate with Heaven, start by making the effort to reach the peak of your own inner being. Remain there as long as possible, tasting the intensity of life at that level, then, after a few moments — for it is difficult to sustain this intensity for long — let yourself go, let yourself be born away on light as though you were floating on the calm surface of the ocean, thinking of nothing

...feeling almost nothing. When you do this you will no longer be in danger, for it is your living, vibrant soul that takes charge and is there, steeping itself in all the purest, most luminous elements. And, when you are obliged to come back to the humdrum tasks of daily life, you will feel that those spiritual elements have restored and harmonized every part of you. You can feel that your will to work and your desire to help and love others are strengthened, and this is a sensation that cannot lie. There : it is very simple ; very clear.

Chapter Five

SHOULD WE CONSULT CLAIRVOYANTS ?

A great many people imagine that spirituality consists almost exclusively in reading a few occult books, attending an occasional spiritualistic seance and consulting clairvoyants in order to learn about their future or their past lives. Well, as far as clairvoyants go, there is never any shortage ; there are swarms of them ! There are thousands and thousands of people in the world who claim to be mediums or exceptionally lucid clairvoyants and who put notices in the newspapers, advertising their horoscopes or their talismans and gems that will enable you to obtain everything your heart desires : happiness, wealth, love and luck. Personally, I believe that there are a few really great clairvoyants in the world. As for all the others ...you can forget about them !

No one believes more strongly in clairvoyance than I do, and I am delighted to see that science

is beginning to admit that there are human beings
with powers of extra-sensorial perception and that
it is beginning to study the phenomenon. As far as
I am concerned, however, the question is not
whether to doubt or to believe in these things but
to find the best methods to help us to make progress in the spiritual life ; and by the best methods
I mean the least dangerous and most effective,
which, although they may be the slowest, are the
most enduring. The sad thing is that people are in
such a hurry ; they have neither the faith nor the
patience to commit themselves to the slower but
surer methods of light. They are in a hurry to
become clairvoyants in the same way as they might
become manicurists or chiropodists. Also, as soon
as they have a glimmering of success, they blow it
up out of all proportion in order to attract clients
and lead a great many people astray by taking advantage of their gullibility and lack of discernment.

A lot of men and women have chosen the pro-
fession of clairvoyant or medium because they were
incapable of doing anything else ! I have known a
great many like that. For years I saw them trying
first one job then another without success and then,
one day, I learned to my amazement that they had
set up as clairvoyants, fortune-tellers or diviners.
They live just anyhow, they exercise no self-
discipline, and they call themselves clairvoyants !
And this is what so many people do : on the strength

of a couple of lucky presentiments or one or two premonitory dreams, they set themselves up as clairvoyants. I don't deny that they may have a smattering of psychic gifts and faculties, a little intuition and a certain sensitivity to the invisible world, but they certainly have an abundance of cunning and impudence. They have understood that human beings need to be reassured and flattered and they tell them whatever they want to hear.

Sometimes, in fact, they see nothing at all but, as they don't want to disappoint a client or lose their reputation — or, simply, because they don't want to lose money — they fob people off with vague answers calculated not to compromise them in any way. Not many clairvoyants are sufficiently honest to tell you frankly, 'I'm sorry, I can't tell you anything today because I can't see anything. You'll have to come back another day.' Oh, no ! They would rather pretend to see something. To begin with, of course, people are inclined to be sceptical about what a clairvoyant tells them, but they always enjoy being told that they will soon meet the man or woman of their life or that they are going to come into a fortune and fulfil all their ambitions. If none of it comes true, it doesn't really matter ...they go on hoping. On the other hand, if a clairvoyant warns them that they are going to have to meet with difficulties and trials they are not so eager to consult him again, even if it turns out to be true : they have the impression that he brings them bad luck, so they go back to one that foretells success. If his dazzling prophecies fail to materialize, they go to him again to ask why. 'Oh, it has simply been delayed a little because of the positions of the stars', says the clairvoyant, reassuringly. 'But it is coming. Be patient !' And, once again, hope and joy are restored.

Believe me, this is what happens. And who is at fault ? First and foremost, of course, those who consult clairvoyants. Since their need for fairy-tales is so great, they will always find plenty of kind, charitable people who will be only too pleased to satisfy them. As for all those so-called clairvoyants who claim to be competent to advise others, to answer all their questions about the past, present and future, and to solve all their problems ...don't they realize that they run the risk of misleading people ? Don't they realize what a responsibility that is ? Why do they do it ? Is it for money ? or prestige ? Whatever the reason, they would do well to realize that the Invisible World does not like being used for selfish purposes and that it will punish them for doing so.

Let me say it again : I don't deny that some people have a gift. There is no doubt about it. But their gift does not mean that they are immune from all weaknesses, nor does it protect them from the entities of darkness that are particularly drawn to those who have not learned to resist temptations —

including the temptations of their own greed. One can be truly clairvoyant and, at the same time, manifest oneself as a creature of doubtful morals, just as one can be a poet, musician or philosopher and live almost like an animal. Some people have the gift of second sight because, in a previous incarnation, they worked to obtain it ; in their present life, however, if they follow their baser inclinations, we shall see both aspects — their failings and vices and their clairvoyance — manifesting themselves at the same time, until they finally lose the gift, just as poets, musicians or philosophers lose their gift if they do not work inwardly to retain it. Actually, the clairvoyance of someone who has no other qualities to recommend him to you cannot be very remarkable. Be careful, therefore, if you are really determined to consult a clairvoyant : don't go to just anyone.

Now, I want to draw your attention to another point in this connection : many people consult clairvoyants and ask them questions that they are perfectly capable of answering for themselves if only they would use their own intelligence, judgment and common sense. Many indications are already there, under their very noses, but they neither see nor hear them ; instead, they go rushing off to consult clairvoyants, diviners and fortune-tellers. What is the use of God having given each one of us eyes, ears and a brain, if we always go and consult other people ?

Besides, what do people hope to hear when they consult others ? The truth ? Not a bit of it : as likely as not they hope for the exact opposite. They hope to receive enough encouragement to tip the balance in favour of doing something wrong. Take just one example : many men and women, who want to leave their partner and go and live with someone who is more to their taste, consult a clairvoyant in the hope that she will tell them, 'Yes, yes ; you are doing the right thing. That is where your happiness lies.' And, incidentally, almost all self-styled clairvoyants would say that. But if they consulted a different 'seer', the only genuine 'clear seer', their own higher Self, they would hear it warning them, 'Take care, my child ; it is a very serious matter to abandon your family. You have a duty towards them. Think about it very carefully, for you may regret it one day.' But they don't want to hear that inner voice ; they would rather listen to the voice of a total stranger, as long as it encourages them to do what they want to do.

Some of you will say, 'But we have to consult clairvoyants if we want to know our future. You can never tell what the future holds and that is worrying ; we need to know !' Well, I understand your anxiety, but you don't need someone with second sight to tell you that. If you only knew how easy it was to know one's future ! Not, of course, in what concerns your professional career, your marriage or your financial ups and downs — but none of that is essential. The only thing you absolutely need to know is whether you are going to advance on the path of evolution, whether you are going to be free and happy, to dwell in light and peace, or not ; and this is very easy to foresee. Let me explain how.

If you have an irresistible love of all that is great and noble, all that is just and beautiful, and if you work with all your heart and mind and will to attain and achieve this, then your future is laid out in advance : you will, one day, live in conditions that correspond to your aspirations, your ideal. This is the only thing you need to know about your future. All the rest is secondary, because all the rest is transitory, it can be given and it can be taken away. All that remains, in the long run, is that which corresponds exactly to the aspirations of your soul and spirit.

If the destiny of most human beings is so mediocre, it is because they are incapable of choosing the path of light and sticking to it : they constantly waver between darkness and light, so their future is always uncertain. Try, henceforth, to channel all your energies towards the luminous world of harmony and love, towards the divine world. A few clouds may darken the picture from time to time, but they will not last long : if you always keep the right orientation in mind, the day will come when you will no longer stray from your course. There, that is the only thing that is essential, and I deal in essentials. If you want to know the rest, go and consult whom you please, but you must realize that you will not learn anything essential.

In any event, you can be sure that you will never obtain anything that you have not prepared in advance. It is a question of mathematics : if you have the three letters, a, b and c, you can only combine them in a limited number of ways : ab, ac, ba, bc, ca and cb. Six combinations in all, no more. Similarly, if you have any special weakness, talent or failing, the situations in which you find yourself as a result will necessarily be an exact reflection of the combination of these factors. It would be useless to expect or hope for anything else.

Incidentally, this is the only way to explain the question of grace. The Christian doctrine of grace is far from making the question clear : we are given the impression that, for nothing more than a whim on the part of Heaven, some people are given grace and others are not ; we can never know why or how grace is granted to some and refused to others, and this has led to confusion and, even, to a sentiment of revolt amongst Christians. The truth is that grace is only given to those who have earned it, and this can only be fully understood in the light of reincarnation, that is to say, if we acknowledge that each human being receives, in this life, only what he has merited by his conduct in his previous lives. He who has already given proof of endurance, nobility, love and a sense of sacrifice in previous lives will, of course, receive grace from Heaven and be entrusted with an exalted mission.

Human destiny, therefore, is ruled by mathematically exact laws. It is important to understand this : your future depends on the orientation of your life today. Similarly, what you are now is the result of what you have done in the past. This is why it is not particularly useful to go and consult clairvoyants about your previous lives ; what can you hope to learn ? People have sometimes come and told me what a clairvoyant has said about their past, and I have often been amazed. A kind, gentle, humble man, for instance, who wouldn't hurt a fly, tells me that he was Napoleon. What a dramatic transformation ! And another, with a very limited amount of intelligence, tells me that he was Shakespeare. Well, I have no objection, of course ; but isn't it all a bit unlikely ? You would be amazed to know the number of people who have told me that they were reincarnations of saints, geniuses, kings and queens, pharaohs and Initiates ! Personally, I have also had revelations from clairvoyants. I'm not going to tell you what they told me about myself, but some of them even discovered who had been my wife, my mother or my daughters in previous lives. The extraordinary thing is that I feel no affinity at all with those people in this life ; I have forgotten all about them. I have often

wondered why I don't recognize my own family.
There are people with whom I have felt an affinity
but I have never been told that they had been my
parents or children in the past, and then, all of a
sudden, I am asked to believe that others have been
my sons or daughters, my wife or my mother !

Here again, try to understand what I am saying :
I don't mean that we must never believe any of their
revelations ; on the contrary, there is often a grain
of truth in them. When someone is sensitive and
psychically developed, he picks up certain messages
from the invisible world, but it is rare that no degree
of error slips in to what he thinks he has picked up,
with the result that what he passes on to you will
be an inextricable mixture of true and false. If you
wanted to know exactly what to believe you would
have to be capable of untangling all that. But, is
any of this really useful ? What use is it to you if
someone reveals your past to you ? If it were really useful, I would have been the first to do it. But,
that is just it : I don't do it. Of course, you may
think that that is because I am not capable of doing
so, that I lack those faculties that others possess to
such a high degree. Well, think what you like ; it
is all the same to me.

In any case, it is neither good psychology nor
good pedagogy to tell human beings about their
previous incarnations. One day, to be sure, you will
reach a point in your evolution when you will be

in a position to do something about it, but you must first be a little more advanced and more in control of yourself. Imagine, for instance, that you learn that so-and-so was your arch-enemy in the past and that he murdered you. If you are weak and unable to control yourself, what will result from this knowledge ? Such revelations are highly dangerous, they can disturb you greatly and awaken sentiments that would be detrimental to your evolution. If it is so important for human beings to know about their previous incarnations why does Providence hide the knowledge from them ? Surely, if Providence has caused us to forget them, there must be a reason. The reason is simply to help us avoid more mistakes.

As long as you have no idea that somebody once did you great harm, you can put up with them and help them. What would you do if you knew about it ? Picture the complications it could cause if a husband and wife learned that their children had been their most bitter enemies in another life. It is much better that they should never know ; in this way, by loving them, bringing them up and doing everything they can for them, they pay off their karma. Providence has chosen to leave human beings in ignorance of certain situations so that they may be in a better position to pay each other the debts they owe. Of course, there would be no danger in revealing everything to someone who was very highly evolved and fully in control of himself, but such beings are rare.

My advice to you, therefore, is to leave your previous incarnations alone ; to hear about them will do you no good ...especially if you are told that you were a particular saint or prince or Initiate. And that is what you are likely to hear from some of those who, in order to get money or assistance of some kind from you, try to hoodwink you with all kinds of magnificent but fictitious incarnations. A great many people are fooled this way. If anyone tells you things like that you can be sure that it is not in order to help you ; it is in order to fool you. If they really wanted to help others they would do better to reveal their weaknesses and failings to them rather than dazzling them with past glories ...especially if none of it is true ! And, even if it were true, the only thing that matters is what you are now, today, not what you were in the past. Why do people make so much of the past ? It is the present that is important and, in the present, there are always some failings and weaknesses to be corrected.

Of course, I know that people don't like you to talk about their weaknesses, but that is just one more reason to have the courage to do so : it shows that you are disinterested. And this is what a true Initiate, a genuine Master does. When he shakes you up and tells you some unpleasant home truths in

order to prevent you from going astray, he knows
that he risks losing your friendship, but it is then
that he shows himself to be your friend, a true
friend. And if, when this happens, you fail to
understand, if you fly into a rage and leave him ...it
is just as well. For what can a Master do with
anyone who is stupid enough to want only to be
complimented and praised ? In order to see what
kind of person you are, a Master will begin by
talking to you about your weaknesses ; only later,
when he sees how you react and how much you
understand, will he decide whether or not to reveal
any of the marvels of your past or future to you.

Chapter Six

LOVE AND YOUR EYES WILL BE OPENED

I have often asked someone, 'Why are you so keen on acquiring the faculty of clairvoyance ?' and been told that it was in order to help other people who were suffering and had so many problems : 'If I were clairvoyant I could warn them and give them good advice.' Unfortunately this is not so ; you cannot help people by 'seeing' their problems or warning them of the dangers that threaten them.

First of all, as you know very well, it is not because you can see a future event that you can prevent it from taking place. Also, as I have already told you, it is often better, in our everyday lives, not to see what is going on in the hearts and minds of other people. You cannot help people if you see things too clearly ; it is often better not to see anything at all. Ignorance sometimes makes it possible for you to go on loving people, being kind to them and wanting to help them.

And don't think — as so many mediums do — that if you feel within yourself the pain and distress that other people are feeling you will be better able to help them. It is not necessary to experience exactly what other people are experiencing in order to understand and help them. It is preferable, in fact, not to do so, for that form of empathy usually holds you down on the astral plane. It is far better to rise to the mental plane and to reflect and use your reason. If you are capable of really paying attention and of listening and noticing the few elements that can be observed in people, you will be able, with practice, to divine their true nature, what they feel and think and what they need, without being affected in yourself. Some people possess this type of psychological perspicacity which is a form of clairvoyance. But when one is content to feel things without understanding or knowledge, not only is one very vulnerable, but one cannot be much use to others.

For my part, I would say that true clairvoyance about people stems from one's ability to forget oneself. To take oneself for the hub of the universe, to make everything converge on oneself and one's own interests and on the satisfaction of one's own desires to the exclusion of almost everything else, is the surest way of becoming or remaining blind.

Many family problems — and tragedies, too, for that matter — could be avoided if there was a little less egoism about. Take the example of a husband who is totally absorbed in his professional or political ambitions and who spends all his time away from home, travelling or in meetings. When he gets home he is tired and preoccupied ; he kisses his wife absent-mindedly, never taking the trouble to ask her about herself or what she has been doing ; he is not interested in her worries or desires. He is so taken up by his own affairs that he does not even notice that she is beginning to change, that she is tired or bored and wants a different kind of life. Then, when he gets home one evening, he is stunned to find that she has left him. He can't understand it ! And what does this blind man do ? He rushes off to ask a clair-voyant whether his wife will come back to him. All the evidence he needed in order to see what was liable to happen was before his eyes for months, but he saw nothing ...and now he wants a clair-voyant to see for him !

At other times, it may be the father and mother who are too absorbed in their own problems to see what their children are up to until they discover, to their horror, that instead of going to school, they are hanging about in the streets or in cinemas, taking drugs or getting into scrapes with the police. If they had been a little less egocentric, they would have sensed the dangers that threatened their children.

Of course, when you hear me say that, in order to become clairvoyant, you have to care about others, you are disappointed ; you hoped for something else. Well, don't be disappointed ; this is the very best, the most useful method I can give you : to listen to others, to understand and respect them and even, if you can, to love them. This is how you can become truly perceptive and intuitive.

When a child is very small he has no other concern than that of feeding and of touching and grabbing hold of the objects around him, of being the centre of attention. If he doesn't get what he wants, he cries and screams and stamps his foot. An infant is a little monster of selfishness. True, but, at that age, it is normal and natural. Adults, his father and mother, know that they cannot expect anything else of him. If he continues to behave like that as he gets older, however, they scold or spank him because he has got to learn not to think only of himself. Later on, he will feel the desire to marry and have children of his own. Why has Cosmic Intelligence arranged things in this way ? In order to teach human beings to think about others, beginning with a husband or wife and children. But how many men or women understand the lesson that Cosmic Intelligence tries to teach them ? How many are capable of really forgetting themselves and thinking of their family ?

As for those who have already achieved this, they still have to learn that the family circle is not the ultimate goal. The goal is to think of the whole collectivity. The family circle, of course, is the beginning of the collectivity — the family helps the individual to forget himself — but it must not, in turn, become so restrictive that it absorbs him entirely. Every individual must go beyond the family, open his eyes to wider horizons and try to be concerned about the larger family of the human race. Just as he loves his own family, a disciple must try to love all human beings as though they also belonged to that family. Only then will he feel a new consciousness, a new vision awakening in him ; only then will he become clairvoyant, truly clairvoyant.

Man attains true clairvoyance only when his heart begins to love. Believe me, true clairvoyance, true sight, resides in the heart — in the intellect, too, but more so in the heart. When you love someone, what do you see in him ? Things that you would not see otherwise. People say that love is blind ; on the contrary, love opens our eyes. A man who is in love with a woman sees her as a goddess — and, whatever you do, don't try to tell him he's deluding himself ! Besides, is he really deluding himself ? That is how it may appear to you, but the truth is that, if people seem to exaggerate the virtues of those they love, it is because they see them as God created them in the beginning or as they will be when they reach the peak of their evolution and return to the bosom of the Lord.

The trouble is that we have still not understood the tremendous power of love : it is love that opens our eyes. If you want to become clairvoyant (clear-sighted) you must begin with love. Let your heart clamour, like the blind men in the Gospel : 'Lord, have pity on us !' and, sooner or later, Cosmic Light will come and ask you, 'What do you want of me ?' 'That my eyes be opened !' 'Let it be.' And your eyes will be opened.

Chapter Seven

MESSAGES FROM HEAVEN

So many people complain that they pray and ask Heaven to help them but that their prayers are never answered : 'Heaven doesn't listen to me. I don't think it even hears me !' Yes, Heaven does hear them ; it is they who are incapable of hearing its answers.

You must realize that the phenomena that occur in our physical organism occur in exactly the same way in our psychic organism. If you always breathe polluted air and eat unhealthy food, your body will be unable to eliminate all the impurities you give it, and the flow of exchange between your body and the forces of nature will not take place correctly. In the same way, if you don't keep a watch on your thoughts, feelings and actions, you introduce impurities into your psychic organism which form an opaque screen, cutting it off from the divine world. When this happens, of course, communication. becomes impossible.

The divine world always answers our questions ; it is continually sending us messages. If we want to pick up these messages, however, we have to prepare ourselves, and to prepare ourselves means to improve the way we live by working on our thoughts, feelings and actions so as to purify them. So many people who imagined that they were hearing the voice of Heaven, have become a prey to fearful aberrations simply because the voice of Heaven reached them through the deforming prism of their lower nature. I have met countless cases of this kind in my life ; truly terrible cases of people who came to me with completely nonsensical messages or requests, supposedly from Heaven. And it has always been totally impossible to shake their conviction that they were sent by Heaven to transmit a divine command which I must instantly obey. Some of them clung to their idea so fiercely that when, naturally enough, I refused to obey them, they went out of their minds. It pained me very much to see the state they were in, but what could I do ? Other cases were less serious, the voices from Heaven had not commanded them to do anything too extraordinary, so I would just smile and let them think that I believed them.

The lower reaches of the moon are, as I have already said, a region of mists, that is to say, of illusions and aberrations, and it is with precisely this region, the lower region of Yesod, that mediums, healers, diviners and clairvoyants, etc., are in communication. I am not saying that none of them has a genuine gift ; my criticism is simply that most of them have an exaggerated idea of their own worth as seers. As soon as they discover signs of a gift of this kind, however modest, instead of telling themselves that they must work to develop it, they go around predicting future events and transmitting messages from Heaven. Some of them even announce the date of the end of the world, and send warning messages to the heads of State !

Perhaps you will ask, 'But don't you believe that some people really do receive messages from the Lord ?' Certainly, I believe it ; the only trouble is that when I compare all the different messages that are said to come directly from God, I am obliged to recognize that they are often contradictory. I would like to believe that they all come from God, but one gets the impression that they come from several different gods. There are plenty of entities on the astral plane that like to play at God ! Someone who is lacking in discernment can easily be deceived and fall into their traps. If it were God Himself who spoke through the mouths of all these messengers, the content and style of their messages, the wisdom they reveal and the advice they give would, at the very least, be compatible, but it seems that God speaks words of sublime grandeur to some, whereas, to others, He says things that are puerile and ridiculous, even absurd. Really, one feels quite embarrassed for Him !

All these prophets, mediums, healers and messengers of Heaven would be well inspired to begin by studying, so as to be better able to receive messages and treat them with discernment. Before starting to say things in the name of the Lord, let them find out where the voice that speaks to them comes from. Before attempting to instruct or heal others, they would do better to start by instructing themselves for, if one has never studied, one can easily make mistakes and fall a prey to illusions. In some cases, in fact, it is absolutely necessary to study the official sciences, such as medicine, for instance. It would be very dangerous to start treating sick people on the pretext that you have suddenly received the gift of healing. It is perfectly true that there are men and women who, thanks to their great virtues and their immense love for mankind, have acquired a magnetism with which they can treat others and have a healing effect on their physical health, but people such as this are rare. Someone who really wants to heal the sick must begin by studying medicine, otherwise he runs the risk of making them even sicker than before. Of course, I am not saying that orthodox medicine is ideal, for its investigations rarely go beyond the physical body, but the knowledge it does possess is indispensable. If you want to pursue the question further and do some research in the direction of other, subtler, more spiritual dimensions, that is all to the good, but never start treating people before you have studied and prepared yourself properly. Here again, you can be absolutely certain that any voice that urges people to flaunt this rule does not come from Heaven.

The various ascetic disciplines prescribed by all the world's religions (retreats, fasting, ablutions and prayer) are designed to prepare human beings to receive currents and messages from Heaven properly. In reality, of course, it is not the physical act of fasting or making a retreat that is essential. What is essential is to effect an inner work of detachment and purification, to improve the quality of one's thoughts, feelings and actions. Someone who has not made up his mind to accomplish this would do better not to concern himself with spirituality ; he would only be a danger to himself and others. There is nothing worse than someone taking himself for a messenger, an instrument of Heaven, if he has never succeeded in ridding himself of his prejudices and partisan loyalties, his baser tendencies. There are many examples of people like this who have ended by imposing their tyranny on their family or, even, on their country. Only someone who is truly pure and disinterested can claim to be a messenger of Heaven.

Everything in nature emphasizes this law : if life
is to flow freely, if light is to pass, if heavenly currents are to pass, the way has to be open and
untrammelled. Why are precious stones so highly
appreciated ? Because they are transparent : they
let the light through. And if nature has worked with
such extraordinary success on certain materials, and
refined and purified them and given them the ad-
mirable colours that we see in crystals, diamonds,
sapphires, emeralds, topazes and rubies, why
shouldn't human beings accomplish the same kind
of work in themselves ? Isn't this precisely what
prayer and meditation are : activities by which man
works to purify and illuminate every particle of his
being until he resembles a precious stone ? And the
Lord, who appreciates precious stones, puts him in
His crown. All this is symbolic, to be sure, but it
is also absolutely real. How many of you realize that
you have this work to do : to become a precious
stone ? Not many, I fear.

As for the majority of human beings, the only
things that really count for them are to be materially
successful, to taste every pleasure and satisfy every
ambition. Purification is the very last thing to interest them. They spend their time becoming darker
and dirtier and, then, when they find themselves in
a terrible state of distress, they are astonished. The
reason for their distress is, simply, that they live a
life of impurity and that they don't even know the

difference between what is pure and what is not. And yet, that is the first thing we have to know before we can sort things out. We must learn to transpose the sorting process that we use for food — when we discard the bones or skin or core or whatever is inedible — and apply it to this other kind of food, our thoughts and feelings, and eliminate from them every trace of egoism, aggressiveness or injustice. This is a disciple's most important task and, since it is the most important, we should devote a great deal of time to it every day. All the rest is totally unimportant compared to this question of screening your thoughts and feelings, for everything else you do will be tainted as long as this has not been dealt with properly.

Even though some people constantly ask Heaven to enlighten them, if they never make any serious effort to transform the way they live, if they continue to be swayed this way and that by their baser appetites without doing anything to conquer them, the answers they receive will be false. You will say that some clairvoyants have a gift that is certainly genuine in spite of the disorder of their lives. Yes, that is true ; in previous incarnations they must have worked very hard to develop this faculty so that now, even if they have let themselves get slack, they still possess the gift. Something that one has worked for a very long time to acquire cannot be lost from one day to the next. But, if they don't straighten out their present lives, they will lose that gift. And this is true for all the other qualities and virtues. If you want to keep them intact you must be careful how you live.

Heaven speaks to us and sends us messages every day, but these messages come from a region in which matter is extremely subtle and, in working their way through the layers of impurities that we have accumulated around us, they become distorted. If you dip a stick into a transparent container full of water you will see that, at the point where it enters the water, it seems to be broken. This is simply an optical illusion caused by the difference in the density of air and water and a similar phenomenon occurs on the psychic plane : the denser the matter into which something descends, the greater the distortion. If we want to know things as they really are, we have to rise by means of thought to the subtle planes from which they come. A dense brain cannot receive the sublime truths of Heaven.

Make an effort to purify yourselves, therefore, to become nobler and more detached ; then, and only then, will you receive clear, limpid, truthful answers to your questions. Otherwise the risk of error is so great that you would do better not to listen to the messages you pick up. In spite of the fact that the modern world gives priority to the intellect and matter, to the physical plane, there are still a great many people who have a certain gift for mediumship and clairvoyance, and it is true that they pick up elements from the invisible world. The only trouble is that the elements they pick up are so mixed that it is better not to trust their veracity. Only the purity, nobility and harmony emanating from a medium can give us an indication of his reliability.

Chapter Eight

VISIBLE AND INVISIBLE LIGHT :
SVETLINA AND VIDELINA

If you read the Book of Genesis you will see that the first event at the beginning of Creation was the appearance of light. On the first day, God said, 'Let there be light'. Light was the very first creature that God brought from the original chaos. On the second day, God divided the waters above from the waters below ; on the third day, He gathered the waters together in one place to make room for the dry land, so that it should yield seed, and it was only on the fourth day that God created the sun, the moon and the stars. But, if the sun did not yet exist on that first day of creation, what was the light that God created ? This was the primordial light, not the light of the sun that we can see and which enables us to see.

In reality, therefore, there are two different kinds of light : visible light and the invisible light which is the quintessence of creation. Some languages actually have two different names for these two kinds of light. In Bulgarian, for instance, we have the words *svetlina* and *videlina*. *Svetlina* refers to physical light and is formed from the root of the verb meaning 'to shine'. *Videlina* refers to the spiritual light and is formed from the root of the verb which means 'to see'. For only spiritual light can give us true vision and, since it was by it that the world was created, it is this light that reveals to us the secrets of creation.

On the fourth day of creation, therefore, when God made the sun, moon and stars, *svetlina*, the material manifestation of *videlina*, made its appearance. And the sun — which is not simply a ball of fire, as people think, but a living entity, a creature endowed with consciousness — receives this subtle, invisible light, *videlina*, and transforms it into the visible light of *svetlina* with which it lights up the universe. So it is *videlina* that, by becoming material, produces *svetlina*, physical light.

As this invisible light, *videlina*, is the very matter of creation, it is present throughout space and permeates everything that exists. Man has not yet reached the point where he can see or feel this light because he is not sufficiently developed spiritually to perceive so subtle a reality. But if he constantly concentrates and meditates on it, he can bring his perceptions to such a degree of refinement that not only will he begin to sense the existence of this light, but he will draw it to himself so that it gradually permeates his whole being.

Christ said, 'I am the light of the world.' The light of the world is the sun. But Christ is greater than the sun and it is this that obliges us to understand that, behind and beyond the visible light of the physical sun, there is another light, the true light that makes the sun luminous : the spirit of the sun, *videlina*. It was this light that Jesus was talking about and with which he identified himself. And just as *svetlina*, material light, enables us to see objects on the physical plane with our physical eyes, *videlina*, the inner light, the light of Christ, gives us access to the divine world. We have to learn what this light is and how to live with it and in it ; every day we must gather as many of its minute particles as we can and learn to condense them within us, until we become capable of projecting a beam of this light onto the objects and beings of the invisible world so that they appear before us in their sublime reality.

At the origin and source of all things is light. And light is Christ, the Solar Spirit. The Spirit of Christ is manifested, first of all, in Chokmah, the first Glory. This is the Logos, the Divine Word of which St John says, in his Gospel, 'Without Him nothing was made that was made.' He manifests Himself, also, under a different aspect in the Sephirah Tiphareth, the sun. Tiphareth, therefore, has its roots in Chokmah, the Sephirah in which shines *videlina*, the divine light.

When you go to see the sun rising in the morning, remember that, when you create a bond with the sun, you are creating a bond with the Spirit of the sun, which is none other than the Spirit of Christ, an emanation of God Himself. It is not enough to gaze at the sun and expose yourself physically to its rays. If you really want to create a bond with the quintessence of its light, it is your spirit that must expose itself to its rays and unite itself to it, fuse into one with it. When you immerse yourself in the world of light, some particles of that light seep into your being and you receive the revelation of divine splendour.

Chapter Nine

THE HIGHER DEGREES OF CLAIRVOYANCE

Have you ever thought about the fact that we can only see the people and things around us if they are lit by rays of light falling on them ? The sun has sometimes been called 'the lamp of the universe', and this expresses the idea that it is thanks to the light of the sun that the world is illuminated and that, as a result, man can see the things around him. And when we are no longer illuminated by the sun, we need other sources of light : electric bulbs, candles, flashlights, floodlights, etc.

Objects are visible, therefore, only when light falls on them and lights them up ; this law is valid in the physical world and also in the spiritual world. In the spiritual world, however, there are no lamps for us to switch on as we switch on the light on the stairs or in our bedroom ; if we want to see something, it is we who have to shed light from ourselves. This is why so few people are capable of

seeing anything on the spiritual plane : they expect
things to be lit up for them. They don't know how
to project the rays of light that would enable them
to see. As a matter of fact, everything that exists
on the subtle planes — astral, mental, causal, etc.
— actually emits rays of light, but of a kind that
cannot be seen by our physical eyes. This is why
we have to develop our subtle organs and switch
on our inner lamps so that we may project beams
of light onto the surface of beings and objects and
make them visible.

There are several different kinds of vision to
which we give different names depending on the
plane on which they apply. On the highest level is
the vision of the spirit ; that which we call intuition. This is not a material form of vision, of
course ; very often, in fact, a person is unaware that
he is actually seeing something. When a man suddenly receives the revelation of a higher, divine
truth, it means that he has projected rays of light
from himself and that these rays have reached to
a great distance and a great height and enable him
to see some laws or correspondences, some of the
structures of the universe. It is the light of the spirit
that lights up the divine reality and makes it possible for man to understand it.

On another level, vision goes by the name of sensation, for sensation is also the result of a kind of
light that man projects onto objects and living

creatures. When you feel things, you vibrate in unison with them, you are conscious of their existence and of their closeness ; it is as though you were seeing them.

And, finally, there is a third kind of vision which consists in an awareness of glimmers of light, colours, objects and entities coming and going on the etheric and astral planes. Generally speaking, though, those who see these things don't understand what they are seeing and don't know how to interpret them without help. If they do venture to interpret them themselves, they are often wrong. This kind of sight is not very useful, therefore ; in fact, it can often impede a person's evolution.

There are different degrees of sight, therefore. The highest degree is that of intuition which is both an understanding and a sensation of the divine world, and it is on this level that we should begin. Once armed with this higher degree of understanding and sensation we can move back to the vision of the etheric and astral planes and begin to explore and study them.

As a matter of fact, there are two schools of thought in this connection : one of them teaches people to begin by developing clairvoyance on the lower levels and, gradually, to work up to the vision of Heavenly reality ; the other teaches that we should begin by focusing on the First Cause, the Source of Life, God Himself, and only later descend to the material level. In my opinion, it is the second method that is preferable. There is less risk involved because, when your mind and heart are focused on the Lord, it is He Who gives you the knowledge of all the different levels of the universe and makes it possible for you to work in them without danger. In these conditions, even if you want to investigate Hell and the spirits that inhabit it, God will show it to you and keep you under His protection.

You will ask, 'Why do you talk about investigating Hell ?' Because the great Initiates are obliged to descend into Hell before they can reach the peak of their evolution. If they tried to avoid Hell from fear of the dangers it involved, something would be lacking to them ; their knowledge of creation would be incomplete. Of course, before attempting to go down into the depths, they must have previously developed the indispensable qualities of knowledge, strength and self-dominance, and, above all, they must be protected by a very powerful aura. The spirits of a lower order, even devils, tremble at the approach of an Initiate because they sense that he possesses fire, that he has thunderbolts at his command. This is why they keep well away from him when he explores their regions and receives the revelation of the nature of evil and all its different manifestations, the laws of karma and the punishments inflicted on those who transgress the divine Law. Jesus himself descended into Hell and set free many souls.

Those who attempt to cultivate clairvoyance by beginning on the lower levels sometimes use drugs in order to stimulate certain psychic centres, and this is highly dangerous. In the first place, because these drugs attack the nervous system and, secondly, because the creatures that inhabit the etheric and astral planes don't like to be watched by human beings and are often very hostile to those who disturb them ; they do everything they can to mislead and torment them and force them to retreat. Thousands of men and women have fallen a prey to the smattering of knowledge that they have found in books. Those who attempt to delve into these regions before having developed effective weapons of defence in the form of light and self-dominance are not only in danger from hostile powers, but their evolution is retarded.

A true Initiate knows that, if he works tirelessly to purify himself and to cultivate wisdom, love and self-mastery, he will eventually reach the summit. And, once he reaches the summit, the matter of his being is so pure that it becomes impregnated with the very quintessence of the Universal Soul, the quintessence on which every phenomenon in the universe is recorded. This is how, once he has reached this level, he has the power to see and feel whatever he wants to know. Thus, his work earns him not only great powers but, also, clairvoyance.

As a matter of fact, it is easy to see that the clairvoyance of mediums is always more or less restricted to the astral plane ; it does not have the power to penetrate the mysteries of the universe. If you ask a medium to rise to a very high level in order to answer questions of a spiritual, cosmic order, more often than not he will be incapable of doing so. But is a gift of clairvoyance that is incapable of raising human beings to a higher plane of any interest to a true spiritualist ? No, it is not, and this is why he pays no attention to it ; in fact, he goes through the regions of the astral world with his eyes closed.

Try to understand what I am saying, for this is a serious matter : before putting yourself in danger by launching into all kinds of psychic experiments, you must make a sustained effort to acquire self-mastery and learn to keep a guard on your desires and aspirations. Only in this way can you be sure that, even in a dangerous situation, you will be able to defend yourself. But if you do nothing to exert yourself, you will always be vulnerable ; there will be nothing left for you but to weep and wail in distress and go round lamenting your misfortunes ! I constantly receive letters from people who tell me that they are pursued by monsters, that their life is a veritable Hell, and, naturally, they all wonder why they are persecuted in this way. The answer is simple : by attempting to enter the astral world for motives that were less than noble — curiosity or greed, for instance — they have attracted the attentions of entities that really do drag them into Hell, for that is what Hell is : the lower astral world.

A disciple in the Divine School is taught that his first concern must be to ensure that his roots are strong, otherwise he will be at the mercy of earthquakes, tornadoes and cyclones. But man's true roots are in Heaven, this is why he must begin by establishing a strong relationship with his Creator, with the pure light of Heaven, so as to sink his roots deep into the divine world. In this way, when he goes down to explore the other regions, he will be so strongly attached to Heaven, that no hostile force will be capable of shaking him. This is the only thing that is essential : to be deeply rooted in Heaven.

Begin, therefore, by developing your potential in the realm of the soul and spirit. Subsequently, it will be quite safe for you to descend onto the astral plane and get to know nature spirits and the entities working on that level ; even those that dislike being watched will be powerless to harm you because they will recognize that you are a formidable power. Not only will they not dare to oppose you, but they will begin to obey you and, thanks to their help, you will be able to do some really substantial spiritual work.

As I have said, it is you yourselves, thanks to
the quality of your spiritual life, who must project
the light that will enable you to see the creatures
and objects of the invisible world. If that light is
obscured by your inferior thoughts and feelings, you
will never see anything but what corresponds to
those thoughts and feelings. The gift of clairvoyance
is given to each one in proportion to his degree of
evolution. If you are still mired in the lower reaches
of the astral plane, the only creatures you will ever
see will be those who are at home in those regions
— creatures swarming like maggots, monsters
devouring each other, wild beasts tearing at each
other with tooth and claw — and you will know
nothing but suffering.

Don't imagine that, just because a man or
woman possesses mediumistic capacities, he automatically has access to all regions of the invisible
world. Not at all : there are different degrees of
clairvoyance which correspond to the degree of purity that a clairvoyant has attained : the greater his
purity, the more he can see in the Heavenly regions.
This is why it is not at all desirable to become clairvoyant if one is not pure and capable of self-
mastery.

If you really desire to communicate with
Heavenly entities and gaze on the splendour of the
Godhead, you must purify yourselves, broaden the
scope of your consciousness and work for the

highest ideal : universal brotherhood amongst men, the Kingdom of God on earth. In doing this, your emanations will become purer and your vibrations subtler, and not only will the spirits of light allow you to come close to them, they will come and visit you, for they will find nourishment in you.

You can develop true clairvoyance only by rising to the peak of your own being, your higher Self. Make the effort, every day, to rise to the level of your higher Self, to identify with it and, from there, to look down at the universe. As your higher Self is capable of penetrating and knowing everything, little by little, much of what you have understood without realizing it will begin to filter into your consciousness and you will be dazzled by all the things that, all of a sudden, you feel capable of seeing and understanding.

The best kind of vision is that of the eyes of the spirit. To begin with, of course, you may have the impression that you will never manage to see or understand anything, but you will be laying the groundwork for true clairvoyance.

Chapter Ten

THE SPIRITUAL EYE

A great many of the misfortunes that afflict human beings occur because their inner eye has not warned them of the risks involved in taking such and such a decision or embarking upon such and such a venture. They set off in their chosen direction and run straight into difficulties. If only they had cultivated their inner eye it would have warned them, for this eye, which is sometimes known as the third eye, is like a radar : it emits waves which reflect back and warn us of the obstacles in our path. The trouble is that our radar is often out of order : our chaotic lives prevent it from functioning properly.

It is true, also, that there are instances when this spiritual eye, even if it is fully developed, fails to warn us ; this is the case, for instance, when events have been ordained in advance by our karma, by the Twenty-Four Elders, and must necessarily take place. In this case, even if we could see or feel them coming, we would be unable to avoid them. Generally speaking, however, if we give it the conditions it requires, this spiritual eye is there to help and warn us and, especially, to guide us. It can only function properly, however, if it is released from the opaque layers of fluidic matter that coat it. I am not talking, here, about material elements but about the fluidic emanations formed by each person and by the kind of life he lives, for these emanations accumulate like clouds of dust or fog which prevent him from seeing anything clearly.

Only purity makes it possible to develop intuition. This is why our Teaching puts so much emphasis on purity, on the importance of living a life of purity, of eating pure food, breathing pure air and having pure thoughts and feelings. And if we constantly have recourse to the sun, it is because the sun is the very image of purity. It is impossible to find true purity on earth, even in water flowing straight from a spring or in rock crystal. Only the light of the sun comes close to absolute purity, and even the light of the sun, by the time it has travelled through the earth's atmosphere and reached us, has picked up countless impure influences which attenuate its brilliance.

Divine light is like a great river flowing from a headspring in the mountains : at its source the water is pure but, gradually, as it flows down into the valleys and plains, it is polluted by all the rubbish that people throw into it. By the time it flows into the sea it has lost its original purity. The same kind of thing happens to the sun's rays, for the sun is also a spring. From the sun flow rays of light which have to travel through the polluted regions of space before reaching us ; this is why, by the time they reach the earth, they are not as pure as when they first flowed from the sun. True purity can only be found on high, at the fountainhead. This is not to say that you cannot begin to look for it in the clear waters of a lake, in the blue sky, in snow crystals, for all these things are a distant, a very faint reflection of Heavenly purity, but you can only find true purity by rising, every day, by means of thought, to the realms of divine light.

The whole of man's destiny depends on the purity of his inner eye. As soon as you do something wrong and transgress divine law, your spiritual vision becomes clouded ; it can no longer warn you or be your guide, and you become more and more deeply embroiled in inextricable complications. Try to become really aware of the vital link between your everyday behaviour and the clearness of your vision. When a man makes up his mind to live an honest, upright, noble life, he purifies himself and his subtle organs begin to function and these organs have the power to give him the guidance and advice he needs to rediscover the springs and lakes, the pastures and mountains of his true Fatherland.

There are important secrets concealed in those words of Jesus : 'If your eye is pure, your whole body will be pure.' People have often thought that Jesus was talking about our physical eyes, but from a physiological point of view that is absurd : the health of the body does not depend on that of the eyes. It would be nonsense to say that our physical eyes affected the purity or impurity of our bodies ; on the contrary, it is the health of the eyes that depends on the health of the whole body or, more precisely, on the health of the blood. Also, Jesus did not speak about 'eyes', but about one 'eye' : 'If your eye is pure ...' It is obvious, therefore, that he was not talking about our physical eyes, but about the spiritual eye that is there to counsel man and show him what path to take, who to associate with, how to behave and how to nourish himself on the psychic plane in such a way as to avoid tainting his blood, his thoughts and his soul with impure, harmful elements. This is the eye that safeguards man's purity and it is in this sense that one can say that the eye influences the body.

He whose eye is pure, truly begins to see, feel and understand, thus making it possible for the currents of the divine world to enter and purify his body. Once the layers of opacity that cloud our inner eye have been dissipated, it becomes an effective point of contact with Heaven and opens the way for divine light to enter. And, as light always has the power to purify, if we know how to expose ourselves to its rays, they are capable of driving every impurity from us. 'If your eye is pure, your whole body will be pure', in other words, if your eye is pure, your whole body will be full of light.

When Jesus spoke of the spiritual 'eye', therefore, this is what he was talking about : the organ or faculty that can give us the vision of Heaven and its inhabitants. The inhabitants of Heaven are, as it were, drenched in light ; delicious perfumes emanate from them ; their whole being sings and diffuses an unutterably lovely symphony. The secret of how to obtain the vision of this sublime reality is to work tirelessly at our own purification, to free ourselves from everything that can darken or degrade us, to allow ourselves only pure thoughts, pure feelings and pure actions until, one day, we have a clear vision of what life in Heaven is and what it should be on earth. For it is not the intellect but the contemplation of divine life that can give us the solutions to our problems. It is by means of purity, therefore, that we can realize Jesus' prayer : 'Thy Kingdom come on earth as it is in Heaven'.

If you are wise, if you are reasonable and attentive you will begin this work within yourselves immediately. And, when you do this, the light will shine more and more brightly : your inner eye will be purified, the bandages and scales will drop from it and you will be able to see, feel, understand and contemplate the divine world which was once our dwelling place, the world from which we come and which is our true Homeland, the Homeland that we have almost forgotten. We must begin at once, without further delay, to turn our eyes towards this world of splendour and absolute perfection. If we contemplate it tirelessly it will gradually imprint itself on the very depths of our being and, even, on our physical body so that it, too, may vibrate in unison with the divine world.

It has often been said that the Church invented moral law in order to exploit the ignorant and credulous masses. It is certainly true that, in many cases, the clergy used religion to serve inferior interests or passions. But true religion and morality are not based on profit. They are based on a profound knowledge of the causes and effects of each thought, feeling and action. The error of the clergy lay in not attempting to explain the rules they imposed. What the faithful needed, in order to advance and evolve, was to know that true morality rests on an exact knowledge of the great cosmic laws ; but, instead of teaching them this, the clergy treated them like children, ordering them to do this or that and expecting them to obey without further explanation. This is why, like children, they disobeyed just as soon as they got the chance !

Try, henceforth, to understand the importance of the link between the purity of your life and the clarity of your spiritual vision. When your inner eye sees things clearly you are forewarned and protected : as soon as it senses that you are in danger of losing your way in dark, dangerous regions, it warns you to go in a different direction. When you feel hesitant and unsure it is a sign that your inner eye is saying, 'Watch your step ; there is swampy ground ahead. Don't go any further. Stop and go back.' And then, when you have managed to get back onto the right path, it says, 'Now you're safe. This is the right path. Follow it and it will take you to the shining Temple at the summit, the Temple of the Holy Grail, the Heavenly Homeland.'

Chapter Eleven

TO SEE GOD

Jesus said, 'Blessed are the pure in heart, for they shall see God.' Why is clear-sightedness linked to purity ? The answer is really very simple : in the olden days, when people used oil lamps to light their houses, they had to wash off the soot that accumulated on the glass chimney, otherwise, even when the lamp was lit, it shed no light. This is exactly what occurs in man : if he allows layers of impurities to accumulate within him, they will form a screen between him and the light of the divine world, and he will be unable to see anything. Purity, therefore, allows us to see things clearly ; that is why Jesus said, 'Blessed are the pure in heart, for they shall see God.'

Actually, purity of heart alone is not sufficient to allow us to see God with our inner eyes : we also need purity of the intellect, the soul and the spirit. In the psychic life, however, our work of purification has to begin with the heart, for it is in the heart, which corresponds to the astral plane, that the impurities of greed, jealousy, hatred, the desire for revenge, etc., first creep in.

Of course, you realize that to 'see' God does not mean that God appears before our physical eyes. In any case, in this sense, no one has ever seen God ; no saint nor prophet, no apostle nor martyr, no virgin nor patriarch, no Initiate, has ever seen God with their physical eyes. Even Moses never saw God, although the Pentateuch often says that God spoke to him. Here, too, we have to understand : it was not God Himself who spoke to Moses, Buddha, Zoroaster or Orpheus. God spoke to them through intermediaries, through His servants, the great Archangels, for His prophets were incapable of hearing His voice or seeing His countenance ; they would simply have disintegrated. You will say, 'But didn't Jesus see God ?' Yes, inasmuch as he was Christ, you can say that Jesus saw God, because Christ, the Son, is one with the Father. But Christ is a cosmic spirit, and if we can truthfully say that Jesus or any other great Initiate has seen God it is because he could do so through the mediation of the spirit of Christ with whom he was united ; he has never seen Him with his physical eyes.

No one has ever seen God, because God is infinite, limitless. It is possible to sense His presence ; it is even possible to glimpse His manifestations in a flash of lightning, a ray of light, but the Author of those manifestations cannot be seen. Our physical eyes are not capable of seeing God : that's all there is to it. For an object or a being to be visible to us, it has to have form, dimensions, an outline ; it has to be located in time and space. But God is beyond the limits of time and space ; all we can see of Him are some dim reflections, a few manifestations scattered here and there in the stones, plants and animals of earth, and in human beings, particularly in their lofty thoughts, their generous sentiments, their gestures of kindness or courage, their works of art. The purer you are, the more readily you will be able to distinguish traces of God, His life, His perfume and His music in the things around you. When you see the sun, you will be able to say, 'I am more intensely alive because I have seen God in the light of the sun, I have felt God in the warmth of the sun.' But to declare that one has seen and talked to God face to face is utter nonsense ! Only someone who is real-

ly out of his mind would claim such a thing.
He who is limited cannot grasp that which is
limitless. He who is small can have no conception
of immensity. When shall we understand the
limitless, the infinite ? When we lose ourselves
in it, when we become one with it. Only then
shall we, at last, have any conception of immensity, of the infinite.

As long as man is conscious of himself as
separate from God he can never have any conception of the vastness, the infinity of God. He
must melt into Him, lose himself in Him ; only
then can he know God because he will be God,
he will have become God. As long as man is
separate and apart from Him he cannot know
Him. But man can never fuse into one with
God unless he gets rid of all his impurities. A
vivid illustration of this can be seen in a little
experiment with quicksilver that is probably familiar to you all. You take a small quantity of
quicksilver and break it up into little drops on
a clean surface. Then, when you push the drops
together, they immediately coalesce into one
again. But if you sprinkle a little dust on them,
whatever you do after that, you will never be
able to get them to fuse together again ; they
will remain obstinately separate. Well, this is what
happens with us : the Lord is all splendour, all

light, all immensity, and we shall always be separate from Him as long as we are vicious, evil and without light. Only by cleansing ourselves of the accumulated layers of impurities within us can we become one with God, can we, in other words, 'see God'.

Chapter Twelve

THE TRUE MAGIC MIRROR :
THE UNIVERSAL SOUL

From earliest Antiquity, seers, diviners and magicians have used what they called 'magic mirrors' to help them to see the past, foretell the future or see an event that was taking place at a distance. A 'magic mirror', in spite of its name, is not necessarily a looking glass : it can be a crystal ball, a cup of water, a pearl, and so on. One of the most famous magic mirrors mentioned in occult literature is the crystal of coal owned by the English occultist of the 16th Century, John Dee. Gustav Meyrink tells the story in his novel *L'Ange à la fenêtre d'Occident*. It would take too long to tell the whole story, today, but all kinds of dramatic adventures take place in connection with this mirror.

Various things can serve as a magic mirror, therefore, even a fingernail. You can coat your nail with ink or varnish and, if you know how to concentrate on it, it can become a magic mirror. Perhaps you will ask, 'But how can all kinds of ordinary things be used as magic mirrors ?' and the answer is simply that any material object can serve as a medium to vision. Insofar as everything that exists is permeated with cosmic life, every being and every object bears traces of that life, and those traces can be retrieved. The thoughts, emotions and acts of human beings, their aspirations and impulses, their plans and prayers, all escape from their author and his vicinity and spread out in every direction. Nothing ever ceases to exist and nothing ever remains hidden. Not only is everything scattered abroad, but everything is recorded and can be recovered at any given moment. The life that has spread into the farthest reaches of space can be found in every corner of the universe : it only requires the appropriate instruments to make this possible.

The Master Peter Deunov's song, *Krassiv é jivota*, expresses this idea admirably : '*Krassiv é jivota na nachata doucha, chto izpălnya célata zémia*', meaning 'Beautiful is the life of our soul which fills the whole earth'. The life of our soul, therefore, fills the entire world, it permeates and impregnates the whole earth, for the soul is not confined to the limits of the physical body. It fills and overflows the body and is capable of reaching the ends of the earth, the ends of the universe. If every object can become a magic mirror, it is because the Universal Soul itself is the true Magic Mirror in which the life of the entire cosmos is reflected. And, since every human soul is a particle of the Universal Soul, every one of them is a magic mirror. It is for this reason that clairvoyants can be divided into two categories : those who find their magic mirror in themselves (their own soul, in which every event in the universe is reflected), and those who need to use an external object.

An object that is to be used by a clairvoyant as a magic mirror must be cleansed of the layers of impurity that may surround it before being dedicated to the forces of light and protected from negative influences. Thanks to the intensity of its vibrations, a magic mirror can detect and reveal events taking place thousands of miles away. Personally, though, I never use magic mirrors ; I know how to prepare them but I prefer not to do so, and I advise you not to do so either. In any case, you must realize that only someone who has found the magic mirror within himself is capable of using an external magic mirror successfully.

You would do much better to leave magic mirrors alone, and learn to interpret the language of nature. Look on life itself as a magic mirror and understand that it is there, in all the events that occur in the different realms of nature, that you will find the answers to all your questions. In order to interpret these answers, you have to acquire a considerable sum of knowledge, and this knowledge can only be acquired in an Initiatic school.

Chapter Thirteen

DREAM AND REALITY

In the past, when country people knew very little about the theatre and even less about films or television, it sometimes happened that a very simple, naïve person who found himself at the cinema for the first time in his life, took everything that happened on the screen as deadly serious. If a murder was about to be committed, for instance, he would stand up, shouting insults at the villain and warning the victim of the danger. Then he would call on the audience to help him catch the murderer before he could carry out his dastardly plan. Everybody else in the theatre, of course, just laughed at the poor ignorant fellow. Well, don't you see that, in many circumstances in life, you are exactly like those ignorant people who took a play or a film for reality : you take everything that happens on the stage as deadly serious.

Everything in life is simply an appearance, an illusion, but when you are faced with trials and difficulties, instead of telling yourself, 'It's only a play. It's not really serious', you start weeping and lamenting and wringing your hands. Instead of moaning you should do some thinking. Let me give you an example to show you what I mean. Take an actor : every evening he acts in a play in which his mortal enemy murders him by putting poison in his drink ! But if you were to meet that same actor after the performance you would see him having a friendly beer with his 'murderer', without the least anxiety that he might slip some poison into his glass. Try to understand that, relatively speaking, the same kind of play is being acted out in your everyday life and, instead of taking certain situations so much to heart, tell yourself that you are watching a play and that you will see things very differently once the performance is over. If you habitually reasoned in this way you would no longer be so upset by the difficulties, failures and disappointments in life.

Take another example : suppose you have a nightmare in which you are being pursued. You run away as fast as you can until, all of a sudden, an abyss opens at your feet and you tumble headlong into it. Your anguish is such that, even when you wake up, you continue to feel the terror of the nightmare as though it were reality. But it is not reality ; you are alive and safely in bed. And you can have a similar sensation with a happy dream : a feeling of joy stays with you, even when you are awake, as though you had really had a happy experience. And now, think about this for a moment : if you can experience a dream as though it were reality, couldn't you also experience reality as though it were a dream ? This is what the wise do. Whatever happens to them, they say, 'I'm only dreaming ; one day I'll wake up. At the moment I am in pain, I'm ill, I'm persecuted, but it's only a dream. When I wake up it will all disappear without a trace.' You will object that, even if you reason with yourself in this way, you will still suffer and be miserable. That is true, of course ; I know. But when people have nightmares, they suffer, too : they are frightened, they sweat and thrash about and cry for help, and yet the cause of all their anguish is not real. They will tell you so themselves, as soon as they wake up.

A great many philosophers and poets have told us that life is a dream. But the fact that life is a dream does not mean that we should imitate all those people who spend their time day-dreaming about what they want, what they would like to happen. Dreams of that kind are not always very 'orthodox' ! It is perfectly permissible to dream, in fact, we should dream, but only if our dreams are divine, only if we dream that the Kingdom of God is established on earth, that all men live in freedom, light and peace. If many more men and women dreamed such things more often, they would be contributing to making them come true all the sooner.

I strongly advise you to live in your dreams, also, but not in the disjointed, aimless dreams inspired by sensuality, wanton desires or sloth, but in conscious dreams inspired by good and by light. Of course, we must never totally neglect the illusory reality of life on earth. If we are on this earth it is because we have work to do here, we have something to learn here, but even while we live our earthly life as well as possible, we must never forget that we are dreaming.

Initiates understand the cosmic importance of creating sublime mental images that contribute to the transformation of mankind. The man in the street does not understand this ; he thinks that Initiates are ineffectual dreamers who are content with illusory visions, while they themselves are wide awake, with both feet firmly on the ground. For them, to spend one's life dealing with material things is to be wide awake. Well, in this they are sadly mistaken : in the eyes of an Initiate, it is they who are fast asleep. Fast asleep and snoring ! Their life is one long sleep, disturbed only by an occasional convulsive twitching.

Yes, life on earth is a sleep. This is why it is true to say that death is an awakening in the next world. But, even there, man is still asleep, more lightly, to be sure, but he is still asleep. In fact, he will continue to sleep until he finally reaches the Causal plane, for it is only then that he becomes truly awake. Then, after a time, when he comes back to earth, he will, once again, sink more and more deeply into sleep as he approaches the physical plane. Once on the physical plane he is plunged into a deep sleep from which he will not be aroused for years and years. Oh, of course, you will see him bustling about and talking and gesticulating — but he is still asleep.

And this applies to each one of you, too ; don't imagine that you are really awake. You are asleep and, just as when you are asleep and dreaming at night, you find yourself walking about, meeting people, talking to them, etc., so in the 'waking sleep' of everyday life you do exactly the same. In fact, sometimes, it is while you are asleep and dreaming that you are closest to being awake, for some dreams make it easier for human beings to be in contact with the true realities. When you wake up in the morning, that reality is, once again, hidden by a veil.

He who considers only outward appearances becomes a prisoner of illusions. Appearances are useful only insofar as we can go beyond them and discover the veritable reality. But to become totally immersed in the world of appearances inevitably leads to spiritual death. Of course, this question of dreams and reality, of reality and appearances, is

rather abstract and difficult ; it is not essential for
you to grasp it intellectually. What is essential is that
you understand how the notions I have just explained to you can help you in your everyday life. When
something unpleasant comes along, remember to tell
yourself, 'Of course, I can't pretend that this is not
happening, but is it really happening to me ? I am
an eternal, immortal spirit ; it is somebody else who
is having this experience. This is an illusion and I
am no more than a spectator.'

To envisage things in that way can give you a
great deal of courage, a great deal of endurance and
strength. Whereas, if you identify with what is happening, you may find that it is more than you can
bear. Those who take their difficulties or misfortunes too seriously get themselves into an inextricable situation because these difficulties and
misfortunes can only be overcome if we begin by
not taking them seriously. Really and truly, believe
me, it is not to your true Self that these misfortunes
occur ; your true Self is above every vicissitude of
life. The entity that is suffering in you is that unreal
self, the actor that has to act his part and go through
all sorts of adventures as in a play. The only thing
that has to be taken seriously is what I tell you ;
not what happens to you.

Whatever happens to you, therefore, however
painful it may be, remember that your life on earth
is no more than a dream. One day, when you wake

up, you will exclaim, 'How stupid I was ; I thought it was all true !'

Man comes down to earth and undertakes all kinds of activities in order to understand matter and, then, when he returns to the other world, even though he has learned a great deal, he is obliged to recognize that he was not really dealing with reality. We are no more than a dream of the divine being that dwells in each of us ; we are asleep and we must wake up. How can we make ourselves wake up ? By thinking of our higher Self, by concentrating on it and identifying with it. In this way, little by little, our ordinary consciousness will begin to unite with the consciousness of our higher Self, our super-consciousness : it is this union that constitutes our true awakening.

Chapter Fourteen

SLEEP, AN IMAGE OF DEATH

The manner in which you live each day determines the kind of night that follows ; equally, the way in which you prepare for sleep determines the kind of day you will have on the morrow. Every evening, before going to bed, take a few moments to collect yourself inwardly and forget about the day's worries and preoccupations. Then, think of any mistakes you may have made so that the spirits of light may inspire you while you sleep and show you how to make amends. Finally, just before you go to sleep, commend yourself into the hands of the Angel of Death — this is what the Cabbalah calls the Angel of Sleep — for each night we die and each morning we rise from the dead. To go to sleep, to leave our physical body, is something we practise every night in order to be ready when the time comes for our true departure to the next world. Someone who is not good at going to sleep will be no better at dying. There is no difference between dying and going to sleep, except that, when we die, we leave our present house for good, whereas, when we go to sleep, although we leave our house, we remain attached to it by the silver cord.

It is important to understand the necessity of preparing yourselves for sleep, every evening, as for a sacred journey, so as to be ready, one day, for the far more decisive journey of death. Many people cannot bear to detach themselves from their physical body when they die ; the bonds that unite them with it are too strong. While they were alive, their heart and soul never longed to discover other realms of space or to be closer to God ; they were only interested in material things, in money or pleasure, as though that was all there was to life, as though nothing else existed. Is it any wonder, then, that they cannot bring themselves to abandon all that ? They wander about, unable to tear themselves away from their physical body or from the people and places that are familiar to them ; in spite of the luminous spirits, the servants of God, who come to help them to free themselves, they suffer dreadfully. Others, on the contrary, shed their physical body instantly, casting it from them as they would cast off an old coat in exchange for a robe of light.

As a matter of fact, the importance that the Christian Church attaches to the reconciliation with Heaven of the dying through the sacrament of

Extreme Unction, shows that the doctrine of the Church is in conformity with the extremely ancient tradition according to which those who leave their physical bodies without knowing of the existence of God or of another world, wander in terrible torment in the dark regions beyond this world. For these reasons, the family and friends who remain behind should not mourn and abandon themselves to their grief for, by doing so, they hold back the dying in the lower astral regions and prevent them from freeing themselves ; instead, they should pray so as to help them on their way.

Just as our attitude as we fall asleep is important for the following day, the attitude at the moment of death is of vital importance for the next incarnation. The attitude of a dying man has repercussions in the next world which continue until his next incarnation, for no single phenomenon, no thought, feeling or action, can exist in isolation ; every single thing has both a cause and consequences, whether immediate or remote. You can see this in your own everyday life : suppose, for instance, that you have had a very good day but that, just as you are going to bed, something happens to sadden or discourage you. When you wake up next morning, you will certainly see that all the good things you experienced the day before have disappeared and been replaced by the impression of something unpleasant. In other words, those last moments outweighed all the rest of the day. Suppose, on the contrary, that you have had a very bad day, but that, before falling asleep, you make an effort to reflect and pray and manage to fall asleep in peace : those last waking moments will cleanse and purify you so completely that, next morning, you will wake up in an excellent frame of mind.

Man is inhabited by many 'workers' who get hold of the forces operating within him at the moment between waking and sleeping and use them, either constructively or destructively. Be careful, therefore ; don't go to bed with negative thoughts in your mind, for they will destroy all the good you have acquired during the day. Before going to sleep, fill your mind and heart with a thought, an inspiration, a luminous image, and you will wake up in the morning purified and regenerated.

Obviously, I am not saying this so that you may think that you can do whatever you please all day as long as you say a little prayer at bedtime, or that you can wash away all the sins of a lifetime on your deathbed. Certainly not ; in fact, that is the best way of ensuring that the Devil will always be with you. This reminds me of the story of a certain monk …There was once a monastery in which one of the monks regularly drank too much. Thanks to his great thirst, the level of wine in the barrels sank very rapidly ! Every evening, feeling a little ashamed of himself, he would say his prayers and ask God to forgive him, after which he would lie down with a clear conscience and sleep the sleep of the just ! And the very next day, the whole thing would begin all over again. This went on for years until, one night, he forgot to say his prayers before going to sleep. In the middle of the night he was woken by someone shaking him and saying, 'Wake up. You didn't say your prayers tonight. Get up and say them at once !' Rubbing the sleep from his eyes, he looked to see who had woken him and found that it was the Devil. Yes, the Devil had woken him, because it was he who encouraged him to say his prayers at night so that he would not feel he had to reform. With this prayer he put his conscience at rest and felt free to start drinking again next day ...to the huge delight of the Devil ! History recounts that when the monk realized this, he was so terrified that he swore he would never drink another drop !

As for you, even if you have not been perfect during the day, it is extremely important, before going to sleep, to make your peace with Heaven. I cannot insist too strongly on the importance of this, for it is during the night, while we are asleep, that psychic forces work most profoundly in our subconscious.

Waking and sleeping ; life and death ; the visible and the invisible ; day and night ...these are questions that you must never tire of studying. Yes, study the deep significance of day and night. Night is the realm of the unmanifest, the invisible ; day is the realm of the manifest, the visible ; and manifestation is dependent on the unmanifest just as day is dependent on night. Before he is born, man lives in the night in which everything is prepared. In the darkness of his mother's womb, he prepares and builds his body, his lungs, heart and brain, etc., and if he does not do it well the whole of his future life will be affected, for the day, life on earth, depends on the night of gestation.

It is during the night that events that are to be manifested in the daytime are prepared, for every material phenomenon is simply the concrete materialization of a non-material phenomenon. This explains how some clairvoyants are able to foretell future events : they see them as they already exist in the invisible world. It takes some time before these events reach the physical plane but, sooner or later, they are bound to do so since they are already on record in the world above. Take the example of a snake : its tail always has to follow its head. The head represents an idea, a plan, and the tail represents the realization of the plan, the materialization of events which already exist in the subtle world.

You have probably all had the experience of being in the middle of saying or doing something when you suddenly remember that you said or did exactly the same thing the night before, in a dream. This is because what we do in the daytime is often a repetition of something we have done on the astral plane during the night.

Every manifestation can be compared to the unravelling of a skein of different coloured threads. Manifestation represents the unravelling of many threads, but only the threads that have previously been wound into the skein can be unravelled. This means that, if you have never used wisdom to prepare something in your mind, it is no use expecting to find strands of wisdom in your brain. Everything that you want to manifest has to be prepared a long time in advance. Make no mistake about it : you will never produce a truly finished product on the visible level if you have not worked for a long time during the night, on the invisible level.

The things I have been telling you today can be of untold value for your evolution. Some of you may not sense this at once, but it will come — just as long as you don't wait until it is time to leave this world before you sense it, for then it will be a little late ! You would do much better to learn these truths before you are ready to leave for the next world.

Chapter Fifteen

PROTECT YOURSELF
WHILE YOU ARE ASLEEP

At the same time as the earth travels in orbit round the sun, it spins on its own axis, making one complete revolution every twenty-four hours. This explains why, in that same twenty-four hour period, every part of the globe moves alternately from night to day and from day to night. While one part of the world is asleep or preparing for sleep, another part is just getting up or already at work. The fact that people are fast asleep in one part of the world, while, in another part, they are going about their business, is at the origin of some very interesting phenomena in the subtle dimension.

When a person falls asleep, his soul leaves his physical body (while remaining attached to it by the subtle bond known as the silver cord) and, bored at finding itself amongst other sleeping human beings, it goes to where everybody is awake, on the other side of the planet. There, unknown and unseen by them, it mingles with them and takes an active part in their lives. In this way, while you are awake in the daytime, you may be visited by many men and women who are asleep on the other side of the globe. Their souls come and whisper in your ear, confiding to you the story of their lives and all their problems and woes. Sometimes, when you feel sad or uneasy, it is because the feeling has been communicated to you by these people. You think that your distress is of your own making when, in fact, it may come from the souls who have left their sleeping physical bodies on the opposite side of the world.

If these souls choose to come to you, it is because your thoughts and daily preoccupations create vibrations that are attractive to them. In the same way, if you often read about a certain country, for instance, you cultivate fluidic elements within yourself that link you to the inhabitants of those countries and — although there may be no outward sign of this — inwardly, you will share in their destiny. Depending on your affinities and sympathies, it is you who determine whom you will associate with and the kind of psychic environment in which you will dwell ; even if you move to another town or another country, you will always attract the same souls and be surrounded by the same atmosphere. If you work to become a magnet that attracts luminous entities, you can go to Hell itself and still be surrounded by Angels and, with their help, drive out the demons who will be afraid of the Angels destroying their kingdom. On the other hand, there are people who would always manage to surround themselves with demons, even if they were transported to Paradise !

You must be constantly on guard, therefore, and, waking or sleeping, do your best to attract only the presence of benign beings. Of course, it is easier to do this while we are awake. In sleep, when our consciousness is diminished, we are more defenceless and vulnerable. This is why we have to be very careful not to go to sleep in a bad frame of mind, but to prepare ourselves for sleep. Some people are surprised when they realize that they are capable of committing horrible crimes in their dreams, things that they would never do when they were awake. But this is precisely because they have not learned to prepare themselves before going to sleep.

The Cabbalah tells us that, when someone goes to sleep, an unclean spirit attaches itself to his physical body and tries to suggest impure ideas and desires to him in order to take possession of his body and avail itself of his reserves of vital forces. These malignant spirits need energies and materials for their work, and they find an abundance of them in human beings, particularly while they are asleep. Why ? Quite simply because, in the daytime, human beings are so busy working and bustling about that they spend all their energies themselves, whereas, when they are asleep at night, there is enough and to spare.

You may say, 'Do you mean to say that spirits come to us while we are asleep and rob us without our knowledge ? But they have no right to do that !' Well, as for that, they just give themselves the right ! Think what human beings have been doing to animals for millions of years : exploiting and slaughtering them mercilessly on the pretext that they needed them to till the soil, pull their carts, carry them on their backs, provide them with food and clothing or entertain them, etc., etc. Do human beings sometimes feel guilty about making use of animals ? Not at all, on the contrary ; what's wrong with exploiting animals ? That's what they're there for ! Well, let me tell you that the invisible world is full of entities who use exactly the same argument in reference to human beings. They have no scruples about exploiting them, particularly while they are asleep and unable to defend themselves. This is why, before going to sleep, it is important to protect yourself by asking spirits of light to guard you.

I know that many people will never accept that there are inferior spirits that can take possession of them while they are asleep. Well, whether they accept it or not, that is their business. But if you want to advance and evolve you are going to have to accept not only that they exist but that you must defend yourself against them. And you can do this by asking for an Angel from Heaven to come and look after you and lead you to the Lord's School where you can learn love and wisdom. In this way you will always have a guardian to watch over your body at night and prevent malignant spirits from taking possession of it.

I have often spoken to you, also, of the image of a train rushing through the countryside at night : all the passengers on board are asleep, as they have every right to be. Only one man on that train does not have the right to sleep, and that is the engine driver : he has no right to sleep because he is responsible for the lives of all the other people aboard who have to be conveyed safely to their destination. And each one of us is like this train whose driver must not sleep. Our body, our physical cells, can sleep, but our consciousness must remain awake and vigilant, so as to continue to guide us through the snares and pitfalls waiting for us in the dark.

As you see, it is not enough to be awake during the day ; part of you must also stay awake at night. This is why, before dropping off to sleep, you must remember to leave someone, an entity, a light, to keep watch within you while you are asleep. Jesus said, 'Watch and pray.' Obviously, this does not mean that we must never sleep, but that we must be vigilant. Physically, we have to sleep, we have to rest ; sleep is indispensable to our physical and psychic well-being. It is on the spiritual plane, not on the physical plane, that we have to be always wide awake.

Many years ago, the Master Peter Deunov gave us a formula and recommended that we repeat it at night, before going to bed. While saying it, place the palm of your right hand on your solar plexus and the left hand, with the palm facing outwards, on your back, at the level of the solar plexus.

Here is the formula the Master gave us, first in Bulgarian :

Gospod văv méné é svétlina
Anguélité să toplina
Čéloveçité să dobrina

Gospod văv méné é svétlina
Douhăt mi é toplina
Az săm dobrina

And now, to make it easier for you to say it, here it is in English :

God is light within me,
The Angels are warmth,
Men are kindness.

God is light within me,
My spirit is warmth,
I am kindness.

Meditate for a few moments after repeating the formula and then trace the outline of a pentagramme in the air with your right hand. Why a pentagramme ? Traditionally, the pentagramme is the symbol that a magus places at the entrance to his dwelling in order to keep the spirits of evil away. Naturally, it is not enough simply to draw a pentagramme in the air in order to be safe, but if you do your best, every day, to lead a pure and reasonable life, when you draw a pentagramme in the evening, it will reinforce the work of the day and you will really and truly be protected.

Some of you will think, 'What do you tell us all that for ? Why do you keep talking about evil spirits, about protecting ourselves before going to sleep ? Why can't you leave us alone ? We have the right to live however we please ...' Yes, indeed you do. I know that. I have no right to interfere with your lives ; you're perfectly free to go on living with your difficulties. I have no objection. My job is simply to tell you things, to explain things, and those who want to do so will set to work.

Chapter Sixteen

ASTRAL PROJECTION WHILE ASLEEP

When one realizes that human beings spend approximately one third of their lives asleep, how can one help hoping that this time is not entirely wasted, that it serves some useful purpose ? To be sure, there is always the fact that sleep serves to replenish the energies spent during one's waking hours, but that is something that happens automatically through the collaboration of the physical and etheric bodies. Why shouldn't the soul and spirit have the chance to learn or to do some useful work while the physical body is recuperating ? To work while we are asleep ? I can see that the notion is new to many of you and, yet, I assure you it is possible ; in fact, it is highly desirable.

If you want to do this, before going to sleep at night, put yourself in touch mentally with the regions of the universe that you would like to visit so as to get to know the beings that dwell in them and be allowed to learn from them. Obviously, these exalted beings will do nothing to help you unless you can show them that you are steadfast, faithful and disinterested and that you are ready to make every effort required in order to be enrolled in their School. The first efforts they ask of you are no more than preliminaries, of course. We all know that students are not admitted to a university on earth without preliminary studies and the proper preparation, and admission to the universities of Heaven is also subject to certain conditions. This is why you should say to yourselves, every single day : 'I must remember to prepare myself for sleep by not overloading my system with all kinds of cumbersome materials. Whether it is a question of the food I eat or of the thoughts and feelings I entertain, I am going to accept only the purest, most luminous elements with which to build my brain, heart and lungs. If I do this I know I shall be always lighter, more awake and more active.'

If you start, at once, and make a continual effort to purify and enlighten your physical body, the day will come when, even when you give your body a few hours in which to rest, you yourself, in your spirit, will be able to continue, on the other side, to learn and work ; you may even be allowed to help other human beings.

Someone who has never had any practice in making his body the instrument of his spirit is not capable of freeing himself for spiritual work in the invisible world while he is asleep. At night he sinks into a leaden sleep full of distressing dreams, and wanders round in circles, chained to his body. You must realize that the body has a very important role to play in the spiritual life : if it is not well trained it can prevent the spirit from leaving it and doing the work it has to do. There is more than one kind of sleep, you know ! Most people would be horrified if they knew where they spent their nights, the psychic regions they went to when they were asleep. They spend their time floundering in the swamps of their own bad habits and coarse appetites. Very few are sufficiently detached to free themselves from their physical bodies and project themselves into space in search of other regions and other beings. To be sure, this is difficult, but it is well worth making the necessary effort in order to make contact with the richest and most beautiful realities of the invisible world.

When your soul manages to escape from your sleeping body, it is never idle ; it moves about, contemplating immensity, communicating with Heavenly spirits and gaining greater understanding of love, wisdom and truth. When it re-enters your body, it brings with it the memory of all the revelations it has received and attempts to pass them on to your brain.

It is these memories that we call dreams. This is why you should try to recall your dreams as soon as you wake up, for, at that moment, the principal images are still floating in your brain. Dreams will sometimes come back to you in the course of the day, but it is better to try and recapture them as soon as you wake up. If you get into the habit of doing this, it will be easier for you to remember an experience or, perhaps, a warning or some advice received during the night which will help you to see what you should do during the day. Some of you may ask, 'But why does this never happen to me ? I never seem to have dreams of that kind.' That is because your brain is not yet sufficiently organized to receive the impressions and images that the soul brings back from its travels in the invisible world.

However, even if you are not conscious of it, these great truths leave their etheric imprint within you and, sooner or later, you will become aware of them. This explains the sudden, dazzling revelations that sometimes surge into your consciousness. They have certainly been lying dormant in your subconscious for a long time, until the brain was well disposed and the time was ripe for them to move onto the level of consciousness : all of a sudden, you are flooded with light.

Of course, this cannot happen unless you have a high ideal and a great love for the sublime realities. The great majority of human beings have no truly spiritual aspirations and never experience any of this. Most of the time, not only does their soul re-

main close to their sleeping body, as though paralyz-
ed, tied down, but on the rare occasions when it
does manage to free itself and pick up a few scraps
of knowledge, it is incapable of communicating
them to the brain. As long as the brain is not sufficiently developed, not sufficiently sensitized, the
discoveries of the soul will be imprinted only on the
etheric dimension (since everything is automatically recorded on the etheric dimension), but they will
not really penetrate the matter of the brain for a
very long time, if ever. It is because the brain is so
obtuse, so impervious to these great truths that they
enter our consciousness only many years after they
have been perceived by the soul — and, sometimes,
not at all. You must get into the habit, therefore,
of working on the matter of your physical body so
as to purify it, make it more sensitive and more
receptive ; in this way your soul will gradually find
it easier to pick up the realities of the divine world
and communicate them to your brain.

To my mind, nothing is more important than
to have a clear vision of the universe. But we shall
not necessarily obtain this by frequenting colleges
or libraries, for those who teach in colleges or write
books are very rarely inspired by the great beings
from the world above. When I read a book I always
question the veracity of the contents, for I want to
learn from those who know and, often enough,

those who know are no longer on earth. We have to seek them out and make contact with them mentally and, then, after a time, they send us revelations and we make great discoveries.

At some point in your lives, you must all have had the experience of waking up one morning with the feeling that something had become quite clear in your mind. You have no idea where the enlightenment came from but it is as though you had seen or heard or understood something, you cannot say how or when ; you just know that you have learned something new and valuable. When you learn things like this, in your sleep, it is because divine entities teach you. The things you learn in schools and universities are, usually, no more than a distant reflection of truth ; the true reality of things can only be learned in the world above.

This is why, instead of trying to devour all the books that you can find in libraries, you must remember that you can ask the Entities of Wisdom to enroll you in their school and learn while you are asleep. When you wake up in the morning, you may not remember all that you have seen and heard, but it will all be recorded within you and, one day, you will be amazed to see how many things begin to come clear. It is important to understand to what extent sleep can be something sacred when you go to sleep with the intention of learning in the world above ; this is where you receive true Initiation.

Moreover, it is at night that a disciple leaves his body and goes to join his Master in order to continue learning from him. Here again, when he wakes up in the morning, he will not remember exactly what he saw or understood in his sleep, but he will have a sensation of something beautiful and luminous that will stay with him all day long.

For my part, I often talk to you at night, and tell you things that I cannot yet reveal to you on the physical plane, for you would not understand them. Nor, above all, would you know what to do with them. Whereas the truths that I transmit to you by thought are already at work in your subconscious mind and, when you are capable of grasping and using them, they will reveal themselves to you.

The day is too short for an Initiate to accomplish all that he wants to do ; this is why he does much of it at night. Even if he sees each person for only fifteen or twenty minutes, he can fit so few into one day — and they come to him so burdened and tormented by their problems : how can he give them the help they need in such a short time ? During the night, though, an Initiate can be in several places at once to help those who need him : his physical body does not move from his bed, but his spirit travels wherever he is needed to help and bring light to others. His spirit never sleeps, it is always active ; this is the difference between an Initiate and an ordinary man.

You, too, can begin to work in this way. Think of all the human beings on earth who are suffering and unhappy, who have lost their way in the dark. You, too, can help them during the night, on condition that you learn to prepare yourself for sleep. Before going to sleep, tell yourself, 'I am going to leave my body tonight and go and study in the invisible world and try to help those who are in need.' Never forget to go to sleep with the magnificent goal in mind of doing some work on the invisible plane, for it is this thought that makes everything possible.

Of course, what I have been telling you can only be applied effectively if you make an effort to lead a reasonable life in the daytime. It is no good thinking that it is enough to mutter a few words before going to sleep. If your day has been spent in a state of agitation, emotion and passion, it is no use expecting to do any great work at night ; your soul will hover round your body, unable to break away.

When you have a problem or question that worries you, you can try to find the solution during your sleep by writing it down on a piece of paper and putting the paper under your pillow. Of course, you must not expect an Angel to appear to you in the night and give you the detailed instructions a human being might give you, but you will certainly get an answer in the form of a sensation or a thought that crosses your mind when you wake up. You must realize that the exercises that I recommend come from a knowledge of the structure and functions of the human psyche. The fact of going to sleep with a specific question on one's mind, triggers certain psychic mechanisms in the subconscious. In fact, many researchers admit that solutions to their problems have sometimes come to them in their sleep.

We can all use the work of the subconscious that goes on at night to help us accomplish our plans and ideas. Is there something you really want to achieve ? A weakness you want to overcome or a quality you want to acquire ? Meditate at length and then go to sleep with this desire in mind and it will continue to work while you are asleep.

I used to practise many exercises of this kind in my youth ; I even managed to cure myself of my shyness by self-suggestion. When I was young I was incredibly shy ; I would walk up and down in front of a shop several times, for instance, before I could bring myself to go in. When I had to talk to someone I didn't know, I would stutter and stammer, and when my sisters brought their friends to the house, I would shut myself in my room until they had gone ! I finally realized that, if I didn't do something about it, this obsessive shyness would be a handicap for the rest of my life, so I decided to get rid of it. How ? Well, I was very young and inexperienced and I would never advise anyone to use the method I used, for it is quite dangerous. I fixed my gaze on a bright, shiny object while trying to convince myself that I had overcome my shyness ; I visualized myself doing all the things that I never dared to do in my daily life. I would concentrate so hard that I managed to hypnotize myself and put myself to sleep. By the time I had done this exercise several times my shyness had left me : I had cured myself. Knowing what I do today, however, I would not go about it in the same way, for practices of that kind can do a great deal of damage to the nervous system.

On condition that you learn to do so with prudence, it can be very beneficial to use your sleep to help you to accomplish certain things. Suppose, for example, that you know that someone dislikes you and is trying to harm you. If you cannot go and talk to him about it, go to sleep with the thought that you will go and see him during the night and tell him : 'Listen, my friend, even if you do manage to harm me, what good will it do you ? You will be happy for a little while and I shall suffer for a little while, but my suffering will make me stronger and, in the long run, you will be the loser. What's more, you will have a karmic debt to pay. You'd do better to give up the whole thing, because it won't do you any good.' In this way you will influence his subconscious and he may decide to change his mind. But, even if he doesn't change his mind, at least you will have learned how to do another kind of mental work.

There are so many other circumstances in which you can use your sleep to get some work done. It is up to you to find these circumstances, to find out how all those hours that you are obliged to spend sleeping, instead of being wasted, can be used to do work that you have no time to do during the day.

As you see, the realm of the spirit is immense, infinite.

Chapter Seventeen

PHYSICAL AND PSYCHIC HAVENS

Although it is usually during sleep that a soul leaves the body, astral projection can also occur when a person is awake. It is not unknown for a human soul to leave the body and go to visit friends in the daytime. Of course, the phenomenon is fairly rare ; not many people are capable of projecting their soul from their body. Even when they are asleep at night, most people's souls remain tied to their physical bodies, so it is no wonder that they are incapable of leaving their bodies consciously, during the day, and travelling to other parts of space before coming back to take up their everyday activities.

You must not take what I tell you as an encouragement to try to have out-of-body experiences ; such things can be extremely dangerous for your psychic balance if you are not ready for them. If you don't begin by purifying and reinfor-

cing yourself so as to be capable of overcoming
every form of aggression from the astral plane, it
is very dangerous to leave your physical body,
because it will be defenceless and at the mercy of
the first entity that comes along and tries to enter
it. It is exactly as though you left your house wide
open, with no one to look after it. So, be careful ;
don't be in too much of a hurry to learn how to
project your soul from your body.

People have sometimes told me of an experience
they have had while meditating : they suddenly
found themselves face to face with something that
terrified them, and couldn't think what had happened to them. It is simply that they had gone out
from their body and been lured into the shadowy
regions of the astral plane, where they sensed that
they were being harassed and threatened. For, don't
forget, the encounters you may have on the astral
plane will not always be very reassuring. If you have
an experience of this kind while you are meditating,
remember that the first thing to do is to get back
into the shelter of your physical body. Don't try to
pursue the experience on the pretext that your
curiosity is excited, that it is something new and
original ; get back into your physical body just as
quickly as you can.

If you prepare yourself for years, paying particular attention to the question of purity — purity
in what you eat as well as in your thoughts and

feelings — and practising many different exercises to teach yourself self-control, self-mastery, then, perhaps, one day your soul will be free to leave the body at will and travel through space without danger. But, in the meantime, don't rush into all kinds of dangerous experiments that you read about in occult literature. Books of this kind claim to lead you on the paths of the invisible world but, in reality, they are very dangerous. If you want an exercise that will help to prepare you to leave your body one day, I can give you one that is quite safe.

On a grey day, when fog and cloudy skies make you feel a little drowsy, instead of struggling without success against conditions that make it impossible to concentrate and meditate, try to arrest all your thought processes and let your soul expand, farther and farther into space. Picture it reaching and fusing into one with the Universal Soul. When it comes back to you it will bring back some pictures of the regions it has seen and contemplated. But don't forget that the quality of what it will have seen depends on yourself, on the nature and quality of your own aspirations, sentiments and thoughts.

You might say that visions and dreams are of exactly the same nature ; the only difference is in the degree of consciousness, one belonging to a state of wakefulness and the other to a state of sleep. You probably wonder to what extent you can trust visions and dreams. Both reflect the level of evolution attained by the dreamer or the seer ; both always mean something, but the dreams and visions of those who have not yet managed to free themselves from the lower astral plane will stem from that hazy region. Obviously, therefore, one cannot rely on them for true answers to one's questions or a clear knowledge of reality. Such knowledge can be gained only by one who has reached the Causal, Buddhic and Atmic planes.

In any case, the essential idea that you must remember in what I have been telling you is that, in case of danger, you must run away. Never stay in a situation in which you feel threatened. If, in the course of your spiritual work, you sense that what you are doing is dangerous, run away ! That is the only safe thing to do and everything in nature gives us the example.

If you find a mole creeping about in your garden and try to catch it, it will immediately run into its underground burrow, because that is where it feels safe. How does it know that it can escape from you by hiding in a hole in the ground ? Similarly, if you try to catch a fish, an insect or any other animal, it will slip away and hide under a rock, in a bush, under a leaf or the bark of a tree. Birds escape by flying away. As for human beings, depending on the danger that threatens them, they will try to escape into a cave or up onto the roof, or by climbing a tree or taking to the water. But the dangers that threaten human beings are not only physical, they can also be psychic. When we are being pursued on the astral plane, in the regions inhabited by monsters and malicious entities, we must run back, as fast as we can, into our physical body, in other words, into our burrow, our cave. This is what happens when we have a nightmare : we escape by waking up, because, by re-entering our body, we re-enter a different world.

You must all have had nightmares, and you have probably noticed that they usually end abruptly, when you wake up with a start and a sensation of immense relief to find yourself in the safety of your own bed. You say to yourself, 'Thank goodness it was only a dream !' In reality, the safe refuge is not your bed nor your room : it is your physical body. And the abrupt awakening was caused by the fact that you knew, subconsciously, that in order to defend yourself against the hostile forces and entities of the astral world, you had to flee to the shelter of your body which was a fortress in which you could take refuge. If you had stayed on the astral plane you would have continued to be at the mercy of your aggressors ; by leaving that plane and taking shelter behind the thick, solid walls of your physical body, you escape from them. Spirits are not given access to all planes, they have been created to live and work on one particular plane. The entities of the astral plane, therefore, cannot pursue us wherever we go ; if we know how to move from one plane to another we shall be safe. In fact, it is this ability to move from one plane to another that gives man his superiority.

One day you may be sad and discouraged and feeling that the whole world is against you and, then, you fall asleep, that is to say, you rise to a higher plane, and when you wake up you can feel that everything has changed. What has happened to change things ? You ran away, that's all, and your pursuers were unable to follow you. If you are being persecuted on the physical plane, you can escape onto the astral plane, and if you are being pursued on the astral plane, you can always go back into the haven of your physical body.

You will be spared a great deal of suffering if you know how to change from one region to another. If you are sad or discouraged, try to go somewhere else to get away from those feelings. If it is your intellect that is tormented, run to the heart. If you are pursued in both the heart and the intellect, go up to your soul. And, if you are still pursued, even in your soul, take refuge in your spirit, for, once you are in your spirit, nothing can touch you.

Chapter Eighteen

THE SOURCES OF INSPIRATION

Let's suppose that you have to give a public address : the best possible conditions have been prepared, your speech is ready, the hall is magnificent, everything is beautifully under control. You talk and talk, but you can feel that your words are making no impression on your audience. Something is lacking and you don't know what it is. Then, all of a sudden, a force, a powerful current, takes hold of you. You no longer need to refer to your notes ; ideas and the words to express them come to mind spontaneously ; your gestures and your tone of voice become extraordinarily expressive, and your audience is swept off its feet ! Yes, things like this do, sometimes, happen. And, even if you have never had occasion to speak in public, you will surely have had the experience when talking to friends : without warning you suddenly find yourself carried away as though you had been stung by a wasp — a wasp from Heaven, of course ! You are astonished to find that everything becomes easy ; it is as though someone else, someone wiser and more radiant than you, were expressing himself.

Of course, this kind of thing is experienced more often by artists, actors and musicians. It is not enough for an actor, for example, to know his part by heart or to deliver every word and make every gesture exactly as he has rehearsed them ; if he is not gripped by that unknown power that we call inspiration, nothing will emanate from him, no radiance, no light, no perfume, and the audience will be unmoved.

Those whom we call geniuses are beings who can, more easily and naturally than others, put themselves under the influence of that higher psychic force, inspiration. But every human being has the power to receive inspiration, although in varying degrees, if only the inspiration that enables them to declare their love to their sweetheart — unless, of course, as sometimes happens, it is just the opposite and they find themselves tongue-tied, stammering and trembling while they struggle to find words that refuse to come.

The fact is that, left to his own resources, man is not really capable of producing works of genius ; he needs to call on another nature within himself in order to communicate with the world of the soul and spirit which is the source of all strength, light and beauty. It is important, therefore, to know the conditions that are conducive to inspiration, conditions not only on the physical plane, but also on the astral and mental planes. For inspiration will not come to you by chance.

You may say that you have sometimes received inspirations in the most unlikely circumstances, conditions or positions. That may well happen, of course. It may also happen that, even when all the ideal conditions for receiving inspiration are present, you receive nothing. Inspiration will not necessarily come to you because you sit in the lotus position with your eyes closed, wreathed in clouds of incense. This is not the kind of conditions I am talking about. The first condition for inspiration is the way you live. It is the way you live that prepares the ground for inspiration.

It is no use thinking that you will receive inspiration if you let yourself live just anyhow, with no concern for the purity of your thoughts, feelings and actions. True, inspiration comes suddenly, without warning, often when one least expects it, but it only comes to those who, in one way or another, have prepared themselves to receive it. Nothing, neither good nor evil, happens by chance. A man who believes himself to be perfectly healthy can, all of a sudden, be laid low by a heart attack. But that is not a question of chance, any more than it is a question of chance when a house or a bridge falls down, or an avalanche occurs. No event in life happens by chance, even if no visible sign has warned of its coming.

Nowadays, of course, people use all kinds of means, such as drugs and alcohol, to give them inspiration. In point of fact, though, what they experience is excitation rather than inspiration. When I speak of inspiration I am referring exclusively to the forces, currents and entities of a very high order that may be attracted to someone, thanks to his hard work and his noble aspirations and which make their way through his mental centres, seeking to express themselves ; this is how the greatest masterpieces of thought and art are born. Neither alcohol nor drugs can ever attract the spark of inspiration.

In any case, it is not because someone is moved by a very powerful psychic current which has a magnetic effect on an audience, that one can say that he is truly 'inspired' ; to be in a position to say that, it is essential to know the source of the inspiration. Take the example I mentioned earlier of the public speaker. A man may well have the power to electrify a crowd of people and hold them in the hollow of his hand, but this does not necessarily mean that he is 'inspired' in the sense in which the Initiates understand inspiration. We have already seen this kind of power in so many political leaders : there is no denying that they have a gift, but their gift is no more than an extension and amplification of certain psychic forces and energies which are often of a very inferior nature. The sentiments and thoughts expressed are perfectly ordinary, but they are expressed with extraordinary intensity. It is merely the intensity, the quantity, therefore, which is enhanced ; not the quality. True inspiration, on the other hand, enhances quality because it introduces purer, more subtle elements. True inspiration is divine inspiration.

This is why it is important, also, to distinguish between inspiration and certain forms of mystical delirium. Someone who is truly in communication with Heaven can receive only currents of light, harmony and peace. All those who claim to be inspired by Heaven and who roll their eyes and utter interminable and incoherent discourses, who gesticulate wildly or remain frozen for hours on end in supposedly ecstatic postures, are sick and unbalanced. Even if they talk about Heaven, the Holy Spirit or the Angels and Archangels, the truth is that they are sick. The whole pattern of their behaviour soon makes this obvious. They believe that they are in communication with the divine world whereas, in fact, through a lack of work and inner discipline, they have only succeeded in communicating with the subterranean regions of the astral plane. From those regions, to be sure, they receive messages and instructions, but they are messages and instructions that they would do better to distrust.

Plato also studied these problems of inspiration and spoke of four forms of 'frenzy' or 'madness'. The first was the 'prophetic frenzy', which was manifested, for instance, by the Pythia of Delphi or the Sibylls. In their ordinary state of mind, these women knew nothing, they could foretell nothing ; it was only when the god took possession of them that they were able to prophesy and warn of future events. Secondly, there was the 'healing frenzy' which gave the power to know which purification rites and prayers to use in order to deliver people from illness and misfortune, both individual and collective. Thirdly there was the 'creative frenzy' by means of which the Muses inspired musicians, poets and artists in general, and, finally, there was the 'madness of love' which was inspired by the beauty perceived in a human countenance or a perfect body. Of course, we must understand that, to Plato, the words 'frenzy' and 'madness' did not have exactly the same reality as they have for us, today. We sometimes have the occasion, in our everyday lives, to meet people who are insane or frenzied, but not, unfortunately, in the Platonic sense of the words !

We can only say that someone is truly inspired if he has succeeded in developing his higher bodies and is in communication with the currents and entities of the Causal, Buddhic and Atmic planes.

In a previous talk, I explained that those who had attained the Causal plane were geniuses ; those who had reached the Buddhic plane were saints, and those who had reached the summit, that is to say, the Atmic plane, were the great spiritual Masters (see Figure 3).

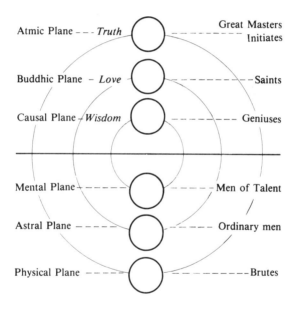

Figure 3

A genius, therefore, is someone who has reached the Causal plane, the higher mental plane, and, depending on his inner dispositions, he receives from this region elements that enable him to make discoveries in the fields of science or thought, or to become a creator in the field of art. A saint is someone who has reached the Buddhic plane ; he is in communion with the love of God and is capable of manifesting it to those around him. As for the great Masters, who have reached an even higher level than geniuses and saints, they have succeeded in melting into the divine consciousness where they receive knowledge and the supreme powers.

Geniuses are inspired beings, creators, but their lives are rarely examples of sanctity ; very often, in fact, rather the contrary. Thanks to their work in previous incarnations, they have obtained the gifts that they manifest today, but if they are not careful, if they allow themselves to live in the lower regions of consciousness, they will lose those gifts.

Saints may bequeath no masterpieces, no creative works of art, to posterity, but they live lives of purity, lives that are nourished by the divine love that radiates from them.

The great Masters, on the other hand, lead the pure, dedicated lives of the saints and, at the same time, are as creative as geniuses. The great difference is that their creations are not poems or symphonies or paintings : the work of art that a great Master sets out to create is a new humanity. By working patiently and tirelessly on the heart, mind, soul and spirit of human beings, he makes it possible for them gradually to advance on the path of evolution.

Chapter Nineteen

SENSATION IS PREFERABLE TO VISION

Very few people are aware of the dangers involved in trying to cultivate powers of clairvoyance. They rush blindly at it because it is something new and original, and it is exciting to explore a realm which is a sealed book to most human beings, to see things that others cannot see ! Unfortunately for the foolhardy, they will never have to look far to find all kinds of people and books ready and willing to help them to satisfy their curiosity.

There is no denying that there are a great many methods for developing clairvoyance, but that is no reason to apply these methods without discrimination. Some people, for instance, are bent on learning how to have out-of-body experiences through astral projection ; they don't realize that, if they have not prepared themselves properly, other spirits will take advantage of their absence from their body to enter and take possession of them. Then they will

no longer be masters in their own home and all kinds
of disruptions and complications will ensue.

Others are eager to develop their chakras by
lengthy exercises in concentration and respiration.
Of course, such exercises will always get results, but
what kind of results ? If you try to awaken your
chakras without having studied and prepared
yourself beforehand, the results of your efforts can
only be detrimental to you. What kind of results
can you expect if you give a baby a box of matches ?
More than likely he will set himself on fire. Well,
let me tell you that the Kundalini force that you are
attempting to set in motion in order to awaken your
chakras is a veritable fire, and that if you trigger
it before you have worked sufficiently to cultivate
purity and self-dominance, you run the risk of
seeing the fire of Kundalini rage out of control and
utterly destroy you. Whereas, when you begin by
working to obtain purity and self-dominance, you
are also working indirectly on your chakras which
will gradually awaken and start to function without
endangering you in any way.

The route I point out to you is always the best
and safest ; if, in spite of all the reasons I give you
for following it, you choose to go another way, you
are perfectly free to do so, but it will be so much
the worse for you. You will soon see whether,
without first learning to control your lusts and your
baser inclinations, you will ever be able to do any

real work on your chakras and succeed in awakening the Ajna chakra which is the centre of clairvoyance. You may acquire a certain kind of clairvoyance but your visions will show you nothing but Hell.

What do you suppose is the first thing a clairvoyant sees when he looks around him ? Heaven and the Angels ? I'm afraid not. He sees the cupidity and greed of human beings, the criminal schemes they have in mind, the hatred they nurse in their hearts, all the dangers that threaten them ...and it is a horrifying experience to have such things constantly before one's eyes. Clairvoyants are often the most wretched of men, and many of them beg the Lord to take away the gift again, for they see nothing but horrors in every direction and it makes life miserable.

And what about yourselves ? Do you think that you will be able to endure such a gift ? No, not if you develop your faculties of clairvoyance before you have developed love, kindness, inner strength and self-mastery ; you will long for the days when you could see nothing, for then, even if you lived in a state of illusion, you were a thousand times better off. On the other hand, if you have already overcome many of your failings, if you have prepared and purified yourselves, if you are in control of yourselves and are full of love for your fellow men, when you are obliged to see evil (and it is impossible not to see it), thanks to your love and courage and self-control, you will not be shaken, you will be moved neither to terror nor to despair, and you may even be able to help people with your thoughts.

Don't be in a hurry to become clairvoyant because it will certainly cause you great distress and even a terrible feeling of revulsion at having to live among human beings. So it is not something that is highly desirable. Just as it is not highly desirable to have a very acute sense of smell. Fortunately, this is one of man's less well developed senses ; if it were not so, people would be unable to bear the proximity of others because of the nauseating smell caused by the disastrous way they eat, live and think.

As long as you are not ready and able to conquer reactions of disgust or terror, you had better not try to see. Besides, one wonders why some people are so eager to 'see', as though it were the be all and end all of the spiritual life. Why is it considered so extraordinary to be able to see the making or unmaking of fortunes, future marriages or divorces, friends, enemies and illnesses. It is always the same old catalogue of human weaknesses : what is the point of developing special faculties in order to see that ? Don't you think that you already see enough with your physical eyes ? We are so often sick and tired of what we see : why wear yourselves out and make yourselves ill by trying to see even more ? Is that an intelligent way to behave ? 'I want to be able to see things', people say. But to see what ? That is the question. Get it into your heads that the gift of clairvoyance will hinder your evolution if you develop it before the time is ripe, that is to say, before you have developed the qualities that will enable you to do something useful with what you see. It is not enough to see ; you must be capable not only of grasping and understanding what Heaven reveals to you, but also of facing up to the sight of Hell without being overcome by it.

For my part, I realized a long time ago that I did not have much to gain from being clairvoyant, on the contrary, so I have never tried to cultivate the gift. This is why I don't see things. But I feel them ; I feel colours, currents and entities but I see nothing. I prefer not to spend my energies in trying to see things, but, rather, to work at feeling, at sensing Heaven and the presence of something beautiful and intense.

A faculty more powerful than vision exists, and that is the faculty of feeling or sensation. After all, the only veritable reality for man is what he feels ; the Lord alone knows to what extent other things, external realities, are real to someone. It is no use telling a person who is tortured by the conviction that he is being hounded and persecuted, that it is all an illusion. Even if, in fact, no one is persecuting him, what he feels is not an illusion. And how can you convince someone who experiences ecstasy and illuminations even when his external conditions are terrible, that it is not true ? The pain and the joy that a man experiences are, perhaps, the only things of which he never doubts. He can doubt the evidence of his eyes, his ears or his sense of touch, but he can never doubt the reality of what he feels. A person's inner sensations will always mean more to him than vision. Thanks to those sensations, he is at the heart of things, he actually touches them, he 'lives' them.

So many people see something beautiful and feel exactly nothing. They see a sunrise, which is one of the most beautiful spectacles nature has to offer, and they feel nothing. What is to be gained from seeing it, in that case ? What good would it be to you if Heaven lay open before your eyes and you felt nothing at the sight of all that splendour ? Whereas, if you feel the presence of Heaven it is as though it were within you : you don't even need to see it. It is more important, therefore, to cultivate your sensitivity to the divine world than to develop the faculty of clairvoyance. When you *feel* Heaven, when you *feel* peace, when you *feel* joy or purity, you are experiencing true reality. What more can you ask for ?

Try to understand what I am saying : the things we see and touch, the things we believe to be close to us are, in reality, very far away. Only the things that are within us are close. This is why true clairvoyance lies in a deep, inward sensation, not in the vision of something outside us.

Believe me, I am not here to prevent you from developing your potential in every possible area. I have no desire to prevent you from acquiring clairvoyance, the power to heal, to prophesy, to command the elements, or even to transmute lead into gold, if you are capable of doing so. I have nothing against these things. The only goal of my work is to enable you to evolve to the fullest possible extent. However, my ways will not necessarily correspond exactly to what you understand or hope for, nor to what you may have read in certain books (whether ancient or modern, many of these books are extremely dangerous). I know that the philosophy I bring you will not always be very appetizing but, if you take it to heart and apply it, the results will be divine. This is what you don't understand, and the reason why you don't understand is that you are interested in everything except the one thing that is essential : to learn to live. Only when you have learned to live will you be in a position to cultivate a talent for healing, clairvoyance, astrology, the Cabbalah, alchemy, etc. As long as this question of life is not settled, whatever you do, you will always be vulnerable to every kind of danger.

Now, I would like to add this : clairvoyance is a gift which can be given to certain people, just as others may receive a gift for mathematics or music. If you have received this gift, you must try to protect it so that it can help you continually to draw closer to Heaven, and, in order to protect it, you must work to cultivate purity : purity in your thoughts, feelings and actions.

But that is not all : your gift will be better protected if you talk about it as little as possible to others. If you have been given the grace of being in touch with the divine world and of communicating with — and, even, seeing — luminous beings, don't talk about it. In the first place, there is always the danger that some people may misunderstand you and even think you are insane. Live this divine life and say nothing. Why talk about it ? Make the most of your blessings and distribute the overflow to others, but never let people know where it comes from.

The other reason for not talking about it is that, as soon as people know that someone has the gift of clairvoyance, they inevitably besiege him with questions of all kinds, from the most prosaic to the most criminal. Men and women will want you to tell them if they are going to win the election or be appointed as minister, whether their husband or wife is unfaithful to them, whether they should emigrate in order to make more money, whether they will soon be rid of a rival, whether the death of a relative is going to bring them a fortune, etc., etc. And what will become of you, in the midst of all that ? When people ceaselessly drag you down to the level of their most mundane concerns, do you think that you will often find the strength to detach yourself from them and be free to savour the things of Heaven ? No, unfortunately, you won't ; and you will lose your light and your inspiration, you will lose everything that gave meaning to your life. You must take great care of this faculty, therefore, for it is a gift from Heaven, and your silence will enable you to help others far more than if you revealed all kinds of things to them about their financial fortunes, their love affairs or their hopes of a rich inheritance.

It is time people understood what an Initiatic school really is. Far too many still think that it is a place in which to acquire clairvoyance, magic powers and all sorts of fantastic faculties that will enable them to satisfy their desires and ambitions. But that is not it at all ! The true purpose of an Initiatic school is to lead human beings to committing themselves to work ceaselessly for the Kingdom of God on earth, for the reign of brotherhood amongst men. You don't need to be a clairvoyant or to possess any special powers to commit yourself to this work ; all you need is to become wiser, purer and more disinterested, and to acquire greater mastery of yourself.

By the same author
(translated from the French)

'Complete Works' Collection

Brochures :
New Presentation

By the same author:

Life Lectures on Tape
(available in French only)

Editor-Distributor

Editions PROSVETA S.A. – B.P. 12 – 83601 Fréjus Cedex (France)

Distributors

AUSTRALIA
QUEST, 484 Kent Street
2000 Sydney

AUSTRIA
MANDALA
Magister-Eduard-Angerer-Weg 72
A-6380 St. Johann (Tirol)

BELGIUM
PROSVETA BENELUX
Liersesteenweg 154 B-2547 Lint
N.V. MAKLU Somerssstraat 13-15
B-2000 Antwerpen
VANDER S.A.
Av. des Volontaires 321
B-1150 Bruxelles

BRAZIL
NOBEL SA
Rua da Balsa, 559
CEP 02910 - São Paulo, SP

BULGARIA
SVETOGLED
Bd Saborny 16 A appt 11
9000 Varna

CANADA
PROSVETA Inc.
1565 Montée Masson
Duvernay est, Laval, Que. H7E 4P2

COLUMBIA
HISAN LTA INGENIEROS
At/Alvaro Malaver
CRA 7 - n° 67-02, Bogotá

CYPRUS
THE SOLAR CIVILISATION BOOKSHOP
PO Box 4947
Nicosie

GERMANY
PROSVETA DEUTSCHLAND
Gemmiweg 4
72355 Schömberg
EDIS GmbH, Daimlerstr.5
D - 8029 Sauerlach

GREAT BRITAIN
PROSVETA
The Doves Nest,
Duddleswell, Uckfield,
East Sussex TN22 3JJ

GREECE
EDITIONS PROSVETA
J. VAMVACAS
Rue El. Venizelou 4
18531 – Piräus

HOLLAND
STICHTING
PROSVETA NEDERLAND
Zeestraat 50
2042 LC Zandvoort

HONG KONG
SWINDON BOOK CO LTD.
246 Deck 2, Ocean Terminal
Harbour City
Tsimshatsui, Kowloon

IRELAND
PROSVETA IRL.
84 Irishtown – Clonmel

ITALY
PROSVETA Coop.
Casella Postale
06060 Moiano (PG)

LUXEMBOURG
PROSVETA BENELUX
Liersesteenweg 154, B-2547 Lint

MEXICO
COLOFON S.A.
Pitagora 1143
Colonia del Valle
03 100 Mexico, D.F.

NEW ZEALAND
PSYCHIC BOOKS
P.O. Box 87-151
Meadowbank Auckland 5

NORWAY
PROSVETA NORDEN
Postboks 5101
1501 Moss

PORTUGAL
PUBLICAÇÕES
EUROPA-AMERICA Ltd
Est Lisboa-Sintra KM 14
2726 Mem Martins Codex

ROMANIA
CORESI SRL
St. Dem I. Dobrescu 4 - 6
CP 1- 477
70 700 Bucarest

SPAIN
ASOCIACIÓN PROSVETA ESPAÑOLA
C/ Ausias March n° 23 Ático
SP-08010 Barcelona

SWITZERLAND
PROSVETA
Société Coopérative
CH - 1808 Les Monts-de-Corsier

UNITED STATES

PROSVETA USA, Inc.—P.O. Box 1176
New Smyrna Beach, FL 32170-1176
Web : www.prosveta-usa.com
E-mail : sales@prosveta-usa.com

VENEZUELA
Betty Munóz Urbanización Los Corales - avenida Principal
Quinta La Guarapa - LA GUAIRA - Municipio Vargas

www.prosveta.com
international@prosveta.com

PRINTED IN FRANCE IN OCTOBER 1995
EDITIONS PROSVETA, Z.I. DU CAPITOU
B.P.12 – 83601 FRÉJUS
FRANCE

– N° d'impression : 2268 –
Dépôt légal : Octobre 1995
Printed in France